Thriving at School

Thriving at School

**A practical guide to help your child
enjoy the crucial school years**

Dr JOHN IRVINE

with Dale Fotheringham and Bill Low

SIMON & SCHUSTER
AUSTRALIA

THRIVING AT SCHOOL

Dr John Irvine
with Dale Fotheringham and Bill Low

First published in Australia in 2000 by Simon & Schuster (Australia) Pty Limited
20 Barcoo Street, East Roseville NSW 2069

A Viacom Company
Sydney New York London Toronto Tokyo Singapore

National Library of Australia
Cataloguing-in-Publication data

Irvine, John (John Forsyth), 1942– .
Thriving at school: a practical guide to help your
child enjoy the crucial school years.

2nd ed.
Includes index.
ISBN 0 7318 0849 5.

1. Home and school. 2. Child rearing. 3. Readiness for
school. I. Low, Bill. II. Fotheringham, Dale. III. Title.

155.424

Cover photograph: IPL Image Group
Cartoons: Roy Bisson

Set in Sabon 11pt on 14pt leading
Printed in Australia by Griffin Press

10 9 8 7 6 5 4 3 2 1

Authors

DR JOHN IRVINE comes from a long line of teachers and claims to have been marking assignments since he was 8. Along with his three brothers (Alex, Jim and Warwick) he became a schoolteacher and had his own school at the age of 18. This firm foundation in child development and education led him to become a school counsellor, university lecturer and psychologist at the READ clinic in Gosford. He is a popular speaker and media personality with over three thousand episodes of 'Coping with Kids' now recorded for radio. He has written four other bestsellers—*Coping With Kids* (out of print), *Coping With School*, *Coping With the Family* and *Who'd Be a Parent?*. He lives with his family at Pearl Beach, on the New South Wales Central Coast.

Dale Fotheringham met Dr John at Bathurst, New South Wales, when they were both in teacher training and they have been firm friends ever since. Dale is a highly respected educator and recently retired as a school principal to take up the position of International President of the Y's Men's International service organisation. His role in recruiting and coordinating the advice of educational experts has been invaluable to this book. In part, this book is a tribute to the wonderful contribution Dale has made to the lives of so many families and so many teachers in his 38 years of educational service to the community. Dale lives with his family on the New South Wales Central Coast.

Bill Low is currently the Superintendent, Department of Education and Training on the New South Wales Central Coast, and is responsible for 35 000 students in 70 schools in the largest educational district in the State. Bill has worked in education for 25 years as a teacher, curriculum consultant, university lecturer and principal, and has held senior departmental positions in educational management for the past 10 years. Bill has a real interest in the middle years of schooling and his input in that chapter has been invaluable. Bill lives with his family on the New South Wales Central Coast.

Contents

Acknowledgements

This is a very special production. I don't know of any other book written for parents about school issues which has galvanised so many top educators to willingly give of their time and expertise to contribute. It started out as a minor update of my previous book *Coping With School*, but as we got involved and as the educators started to tell me what was needed in the new edition, the whole exercise developed a thriving impetus and identity in its own right. This book is no longer just about *coping* with school, which is rather negative and uninspirational, it's all about *thriving* at school, for those who want their kids to do more than survive at school.

Naturally there are many wonderful people who helped this book to thrive. I'd first like to thank my fabulous brother, Warwick, and my much-esteemed colleague, Ian Wallace (author of *You and Your ADD Child*, for all they contributed to *Coping With School*. In many ways I'm pleased this book is to be renamed because *Coping With School* can now forever remain a wonderful memory of the times we shared together. I'd like to thank my very special friend, John Riedel, who came to my aid when I was about to give up on this rewrite and helped sort me out. Then I'd like to thank my new partners in crime, Dale Fotheringham and Bill Low, for contributing so willingly and being so supportive in this exhausting rewrite. Both are very seasoned and respected educators and their influence will be obvious in the many changes to this book.

But you will notice teacher ratings and teachers' tips

throughout the book; thanks to the tireless efforts of my colleague Dale Fotheringham and my wonderful friend, Nancy Wyllie, we have been able to include the insights and expertise of hundreds of teachers and early childhood staff. I'd like to thank teachers and/or principals/Headmasters of the following schools:

Avoca Public

Bourke Public

Brisbania Public

Castle Hill Public

Central Coast Grammar

Cherstey Public

Empire Bay Public

Erina Heights Public

Kincumber Holy Cross

Kinross Wolaroi College

Newcastle Grammar

Niagara Park Public

Northlakes Public

I'd also like to thank staff of the following early childhood centres:

Community-based Preschools

Gorokan Preschool

Gosford Baptist Preschool

Gosford Preschool

Kariong Preschool

Kimburra Preschool

Long Jetty Preschool

The Entrance Preschool

Tumbi Umbi Preschool

Long Day Care Centres

Gosford Community C.C

James Mitchell

Kariong Child Care Centre

Michael Burns

Papalya

Terrigal C.C

Woy Woy Peninsula C.C

Commercial Centres

Booker Bay

Glenning Valley

Highland Grove

Hillside

Kariong Early Learning

Kincumber Kids Factory

Koolyangarra

A book such as this requires expertise in many areas; there is no way that it can represent the very best advice in so many areas without the very best advisers. These talented and committed educators have ensured that contemporary issues in education have been dealt with in a way that reflects the changing realities of schooling and society. I'd like to single out the following experts and although space prevents more than a trite summary of their roles, their comments, suggestions and reviews have been invaluable.

JUDY ANDERSON — early childhood education director
LILLIAN BENNETTS — home school liaison officer (retired)
LINDA BISHOP — executive teacher
MAGGIE CHURCH — student welfare consultant
PETER CLARKE — psychologist, expert advice available on www.counselling121.com
PAM DODGSON — deputy principal
HELEN DRUMMOND — special education consultant
LYN EAMES — early intervention teacher
GRAHAM FORD — school principal
GRAHAM GALE — assistant principal
JUSTINE GOWLAND — health promotions officer
BRENDA HAYNES — early childhood education director
CATHY HURST — school educator from Britain
HEATHER IRVINE — psychologist, wonderful daughter and colleague
WARWICK IRVINE — neuro-psychologist and partner in the READ clinic at Gosford
MARJORIE KONG — leading teacher
ROS MCINTOSH — student welfare consultant
ROY MEREDITH — teacher and, with wife, Wendy, very experienced home educator
GLEN MULLANEY — technology adviser
BRYAN MULLEN — school principal
KAREN MYHR — school principal
FRANK POTTER — school principal

NADA POTTER— inter-agency project coordinator
MICHELLE RICHARDS— early childhood education director
GARY STANDEN— assistant principal
TONY SULLIVAN— Chief Education Officer
WARWICK TEASDALE— executive teacher
ROBYNE TROTTER— consultant for gifted and talented
  (retired)
KEITH VALLIS— computer coordinator
NICI WALES— parent of special needs child
COLIN WALLIS— school principal
TOM WILSON— school principal
NANCY WYLLIE— early childhood educator and
  administrator (retired)

But even with the best of advice from the experts I think we all owe much of our wisdom to the kids we have taught and the families which have supported us over the years. I owe so much to the parents who have taught me. Not just my own wonderful parents and my own fabulous family, but every family I have met and worked with over many years now.

Finally I'd like to thank my wife, Jean. Every author thanks their long-suffering partner. Every book demands so much of its authors that other priorities and loves are often left languishing. This is probably my last book and I thank Jean for her patience and support over so many years and so many deadlines.

I hope now that you and your family find some inspiration and motivation from our perspiration.

John Irvine

Introduction

School is not what it used to be. In the old days schools were the clearing houses for all information. Priests and other approved custodians of knowledge would separate the children by age and, bit by bit, year by year, expose them to the myths, mysteries and morals of society. In those days knowledge could be contained within the covers of a book and the book could be shelved higher or lower depending on whether or not the little grasping hands were ready for its secrets.

How things have changed. The monks have been bypassed, print has almost been bypassed and schools are at risk of being bypassed, as a massive armoury of information explodes its way into every home from every angle. Saturated with television and telephones, mobiles and modems, the 'net' and the Nintendo, the modern home can do little to arrest or curb, let alone control, the information being implanted daily in the minds of our children.

So spare a thought for the schools caught in the crossfire. With many competing pressures on budgets and less political clout they're expected to be up with the latest, down on discipline, facing the future, yet going back to basics. It's a huge challenge we've given them as we demand that they provide a curriculum that meets all these needs to the satisfaction of the most diverse and divided population that the Australian community has ever faced.

Education has changed dramatically since *Coping With School* was first written. In this edition you will notice major changes throughout with increased emphasis on the following:

- A significant rewrite of the section 'Preparing children for "big" school', now 'Preparing for success at "big" school';
- Significant expansion and update on the use of computers in education;
- Significant expansion on bullying and discrimination;
- Significant expansion on the medication of children;
- Inclusion of a section on the rapidly increasing incidence of home schooling;
- Significantly expanded section on the identification and educational management of gifted and talented children;
- Expanded section on behaviour management, with special attention to procedures for suspension and expulsion;
- A new chapter on the middle years and their challenges;
- A new section on motivation (especially relating to adolescent boys) and body image (especially relating to adolescent girls);
- Significant expansion on the section on illicit drugs, smoking and alcohol-related problems;
- Significant update on ADHD and its management;
- Significant expansion of the section on home–school conflict, with more attention to complaints procedures, handling difficulties with teachers, etc;
- A teacher's look at the worst sins parents can commit in their kids' education and the Ten Commandments for Educational Salvation;
- Teachers' tips on virtually every issue in the book so parents hear the rarely publicly expressed voice of the day-to-day professional;
- Deletion of the chapter on after-school problems— these issues have either been incorporated within other sections or more comprehensively dealt with in my book *Who'd Be a Parent?: The Manual That Should Have Come With the Kids*;
- Appendices including immunisation schedule, special needs of special families and a countdown calendar of what needs to be done and when, and starting age guidelines.

Two things haven't changed, however — school is still there and it is still compulsory. Experts now suggest that in communities of the future, with the demise of the Church and other community catalysts, it will be the school that will become the hub of family support. Our job is to see our kids not just coping with school but thriving at school. For if they can then the research is clear that school success provides the single best springboard into success throughout life.

That's why this book has been written. It's written for parents faced with the day-to-day task of making school a successful experience for their children. School is here to stay. Our young (3–15-year-old) children are not, but their experience at school will be their launching pad into life. How well we can help them thrive under the strains to their heads, hearts, bodies and souls will be a large measure of the legacy we leave them.

Chapter 1

Preparing for Success
at 'Big' School

No outside agency has a greater impact on your child's development than school. Not only is it the testing ground of body, mind and spirit, but its key role, above all, is as the breeding ground for the citizens of the future. At school children must learn to get on with their own age group; the price of failure is playground purgatory. The research clearly shows that children's readiness for their school experience is critical to their confident survival there.

In this first chapter we look at ways parents can help prepare their children for school: how to get them off to a good start; how to select the right school for a child, including how to choose between public and private schools; and, for working parents, how to balance work and school and when to do what in the lead-up to enrolment.

Preschool preparation

'On your marks — GO!' That's the way many of us start our kids on the school marathon race. There is no 'Get set!'— just 'Coming ready or not!' The problem is that some children are not ready, so they get off to a bad start. Then they can't catch up and no matter what urging is done from the sidelines by parents or teachers, the kids give up the race. If they happen to have a strong ego they are likely to write school off and give their teachers a hard time. If they are less self-confident they are more likely to write themselves off and give themselves a hard time.

Some parents make the mistake of thinking that if their children are bright enough they'll be okay. But in reality thriving at school is as much about thriving in the playground as it is about doing well in the classroom. Children who fail socially find it very hard to concentrate on schoolwork when they feel surrounded by enemies.

Many parents who are not sure how their children will cope believe that any problems in their first year can be solved simply by getting a better teacher in the second year or just having the kid repeat, but it's not as easy as that. Although repeating often works very well with young kids, it's even better to start them when they're ready, to help prepare them so they are as ready as possible, and to talk about the options with their preschool teacher if you're not sure.

The best training for school is a happy home where children have learnt to laugh, cuddle, wait, watch and, above all, believe in themselves. The next step in preparation is a stint at preschool where they'll learn to cut, draw, listen, talk, share, write, stack, pack and manage without their mums. But I'd emphasise that readiness is not just educational — it's the combined preparedness of body, soul, mind and ego strength.

In general children are ready if they can play well with other kids, dress themselves, go to the toilet by themselves and enjoy books and stories. Along with these abilities, strange as it may seem, being able to write (that is, print) their first name when they go to school seems to be the best indicator of reading success later! 'Ready' kids are all set to have fun and enjoy their education. If kids are struggling with these skills or if they are well under average age for entering school, then please don't rush them on to school. You might be ready for your children to go — anywhere — but if they are not ready then their whole success at school may be jeopardised. There is nothing harder than coping with kids who are not coping! Another year at home, at preschool or in day care could make all the difference to their thriving at school. As Michelle, a preschool teacher, put it, 'Another year to ... roll in the mud, remove the garden rocks to find the slaters and build on their social skills in a nurturing environment'.

Readiness checklist

Educational

- Can draw people with three or four recognisable features
- Has some control when colouring in
- Can print or almost print own first name
- Can talk in proper sentences, not just in two- or three-word sentences
- Speech is understandable, although it doesn't have to be perfect
- Can remember parts of favourite books and retell known stories
- Enjoys using a computer and is developing basic skills of controlling the mouse, etc.
- Can repeat some nursery rhymes and/or finger plays
- Can sing some kindergarten songs
- Enjoys looking at pictures or listening to stories
- Can count own fingers
- Knows basic colours and shapes
- Can follow two simple instructions given together
- Wants to learn, e.g. 'Why?' or 'How do you write ... ?'
- Can stay at an activity for at least 10 to 15 minutes

Social

- Mixes happily with friends at preschool
- Has begun having friends over to play
- Can go to preschool or parties without tears
- Can stay within boundaries

- Can share and take turns
- Has best friends and can talk about them in conversation
- Can talk to adults other than just parents and family
- Has had extended periods of time away from parents if there has not been any preschool experience

Self-help

- Is toilet trained
- Can dress self, including buttons
- Can cut-and-paste with ease
- Can open food packets, lunch boxes and drink bottles, and unwrap plastic-wrapped lunches
- Can care for belongings

Tips from teachers

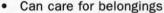 Early childhood teachers consistently and unanimously suggest that parents should not send their children to 'big' school if they're young and not ready — they suggest asking early childhood staff about their children's readiness before making the big decision.

✍ 'One family I remember was intent on sending their son (who was a really nice kid) to big school because he was big, although he was only 4. We advised strongly against the move but it happened. The teacher couldn't cope with his swearing, rudeness, aggression, or his disobedience. The parents were advised to withdraw him so he came back to day care, had a fabulous year and is now doing really well in primary. Every year we seem to have families who want to rush the kids on before they are ready. I just wish they'd put the kids' needs first.'

Special needs children

Having a child with special needs is special! Probably nothing on earth can match the highs and the lows, the agony and the ecstasy, the fun or the fatigue of raising a child with special needs. Education represents one of the biggest challenges — it's all very well having a policy of integration and being philosophically committed to making it work, but it's much harder in practice. Given the increasing demands on educators in every direction, it's understandable that the special needs of special children (gifted or disabled in any way) can get lost, bypassed, neglected or dishonoured. Here are some guidelines to help protect your children in this educational race for resources.

Is there adequate funding for special needs children at the school?
The recent NSW court case (1999) concerning a girl with spina bifida, who won a charge of discrimination against a school that refused her entry, is testimony to the difficulties and emerging issues here.

Is the child ready for school?
Issues here include their level of physical independence, self-help and toileting skills, social skills and ability to mix and cope with the inevitable kids' comments about being different,

5

motor skills to perform expected functions, etc. If not, discuss levels of support and required age of entry with the special education section of your school or department.

What choice do you have of schools your child can attend?
Issues here include the zoning policies of the education system, the size of the schools (smaller ones may be more nurturing but larger ones may have better facilities), and the attitude of the school to having your child on board.

What support will your child receive at the school?
There has been such a rapid escalation in demand for Integration Aid support that every education system is struggling to cope. Check what priority your child would have, what level of teacher aid support the school would be recommending and when they would know what has been approved. Check also what support there is for parents of special needs children at the school or through the school and what the attitude of other parents has been to families with special needs children. If your child is to be enrolled in a special unit within the school, check what support there will be for your child, both in school and in the playground.

What are the transport arrangements?
In most education systems there is a scheme for free transport to and from school for some children with special needs. Find out what arrangements would apply to your child, particularly if you are seeking a placement out of your zone.

How will the family cope with the special needs child being at that school?
Issues here include what support is available to parents, if the child is frail physically, socially or emotionally, and how parents could cope (emotionally and vocationally) with calls from the school for advice, help, child collection, etc. Another issue to be worked through is how the siblings would feel

about the special needs child being at their school.

The calendar in Appendix 2 (see page 241) includes a timeline for special needs children. These issues will be among those that can be sorted out at that time. Could I just add a note of reassurance for parents with special needs children? While it may take time to sort out what's educationally best for your child, virtually every one that I have been associated with settles in and finds a special place in the hearts of parents, teachers and other pupils, *if* the parents work closely and supportively with the school — not picking on the school for its inadequacies but recognising that it wants to do its best but needs your help to do it. I should also add that children classified as disabled tend to have high employment prospects because of the one-to-one support they receive and because of government incentives, so hang in there!

Getting off to a good start

One of the world's leading experts in child development, Urie Bronfenbrenner, has said that children are at greatest risk at times of greatest change. That could mean the change from home to preschool, preschool to school, or primary to middle/high school. At these times their security is shaken and they are at their most nervous. If things go wrong from the start then expect their normal fussing to turn into fears or even phobias as minor problems become catastrophes, and molehills turn into mountains overnight.

So, first impressions are very important, particularly for sensitive children. But for any child a new start can be helped or hindered by what we do or don't do.

DO

✓ **Do** go to the school's orientation days so you and your child are familiar with the school's buildings, bubblers, grounds, play equipment and routines before you both start on the big day.

7

✓ **Do** get involved with your child's school from the start, in any way that your time and patience allows — as a reading parent, canteen helper, homework helper, working bee-er, transport helper, excursion chaperone. Research shows clearly that kids do better at school if their parents are involved in some way.

✓ **Do** make sure your child has the same pencils, clothes, and such-like equipment as the other children — and make sure they are ALL NAMED. The school will provide a list of requirements.

✓ **Do** have 'child friendly' equipment for them. Bags, lunch boxes, bottles, sandwich wraps (stay away from cling wrap, use foil or paper) — all need to be easy to operate by a young child. A bigger bag is easier to pack and add extras to, like spare clothes. Have your child along to help you choose these essentials. Maybe play 'getting ready for school' a few times.

✓ **Do** try to meet the teacher, even briefly, in the first few weeks so that your child is not just an unknown face in that squirming, sniffling mass of uncivilised humanity.

✓ **Do** anticipate that the kids may be a little tired and testy after school for a week or two, or even a term or two. Give them a bit of unwinding time after school, together with time to tell you their worries or fears after you've turned their lights out at night.

✓ **Do** go easy on the extra-curriculars in their first term at school. Swimming lessons, music lessons, dancing lessons may all seem important but don't leave much time for processing all the big new experiences of starting school.

✓ **Do** try to have good breakfasts — I know some kids are slower to warm up to food in the morning but get a good routine and good vibes around the house and get to know what they will eat so you help their bodies and brains cope with the busy mornings at school.

✓ **Do** help make their day more interesting with a bit of lunch-food flair by including the odd cutlet, homemade goodies, a club sandwich, roll-ups or any other healthy but non-melting favourite. If mornings are chaotic then prepare, wrap and freeze their lunches the night before. That way the goodies are still fresh at lunchtime but too frozen to eat at playtime. Consider making up a whole week's sandwiches once a week, labelling and freezing them, to free up your mornings even more.

✓ **Do** be on the look-out for signs of stress — headaches, tears, school refusal, baby talk, crankiness, clinginess, poor sleeping, poor eating. Most kids will show some of these as they try to cope with a brand-new world but if the symptoms continue, or increase after a week or two, make sure the kids keep going to school but arrange to meet the teacher to compare notes and ideas to make things happier.

✓ **Do** remember to take a break for yourself too. Beginning school can be as big for a parent as it is for a child. Use your support network — ask a friend or relative to take and pick up your youngster from school a couple of times a term. It's good for everyone!

DON'T

✗ **Don't** sabotage success by threatening that they'll get the cane if they are naughty or that other kids will knock them into shape. In reality canes have disappeared from schools and schoolground violence is not being tolerated these days.

✗ **Don't** condemn their first day to failure by sending them off with promises of learning to read and tell the time. Kids will take you literally; those who have no idea of time and can't read will expect to pick it all up on the first day and become very disappointed if they can't read to Mum when they get home.

✘ **Don't** forget to let them practise the things they'll need to know to survive socially. If they haven't had practice at preschool in how to cope with group toileting, how to unwrap their lunches, how to ask for help, how to get their shoes and socks off and on, then we can expect the dreaded 'T-thing' problems — Tears, Tummy-aches, Tiredness and Testiness.

✘ **Don't** add to their anxieties with a mind-boggling list of things to remember. Think of all the 'don't forgets' we pepper them with: to eat their lunch, to remember their bags, to play in their own areas, to put their hats on in the playground, to sit in the shade, to make sure their laces are done up, and most importantly, to go to the toilet as soon as the bell goes! Their teachers won't forget, so we really don't need to worry.

✘ **Don't** rush out and stock up on all the school gear in case you 'miss out'. Wait at least until you've seen what other children who go to the school are wearing or have talked to a few seasoned parents.

✘ **Don't** ask general questions when they come home — such as 'How did school go?' That's like someone asking you 'How are you going?' or 'How did work go?' If you want real answers you must ask specific questions: 'Who did you sit next to?', 'What story did your teacher read to you?' If they say they 'just played' then remember that playing is your children's best way of learning about life.

By far the best advice, however, is that, within reasonable limits, it really doesn't matter what you do but *how* you do it. If you are enthusiastic about your child and the school then there's every chance that home and school will make a happy and productive partnership. And whatever you do, don't forget to take lots of photos of your brand-spanking-new kids as they head off on their first day at school. They will never look the same again!

CASE STUDY

Scott

Scott's mother was only 16 when he was born and life had been a battle ever since because they were both trying to grow up at the same time. With no father around Mum couldn't wait to get Scott to school by the time he was 4.

He arrived the first day looking lost, bewildered and sad and also showing strong indications of neglect. When he was asked his name he just said 'Dot' (Scott). On that first day he gave a strong indication that he wanted to go to the toilet so the teacher took him and waited outside. He was so slow that eventually the teacher looked in the cubicle to see if Scott was okay, only to find him rolling around on the floor trying to put both feet through one leg of his trousers. The teacher quickly helped Scott to get dressed and the school began a self-help program to build up his confidence and self-reliance skills. Scott's mother was also asked to become involved in this plan and she realised at last that just dumping an 'unready' child on school was unfair on the child and the school.

Tips from teachers

✍ Forget everything that has to be done and take time out for hugs and cuddles when you first arrive home, to renew family ties, after a day apart. The first 15 minutes after arriving home should be cuddling time — time to relax, to be physically back in touch with each other. That way no matter what has happened during the day to parent or child, they both know there is comfort in the arms of those who love them — and a time to communicate.

Choosing the right school

If a child's first impressions count for so much then choosing the right school can be vital, especially as more choice is now available to parents than perhaps ever before. The best idea is to look at the children already going to the target school, listen to parents and try to get a feeling about the place.

As a general rule schools are what you make of them. And, as another general rule, young children are better off at their neighbourhood school where they can build up an in-school and out-of-school network of friends. Travelling lots of kilometres to and from school daily and then having no one familiar nearby to play with, unless a parent performs a complex shuttle service, can be a bit stressful for everyone concerned. But there are many other factors that go into this decision.

If your choice of school doesn't seem to be working out, for whatever reason, don't be hasty in making a change. Talk with your child's teacher, the school's principal and counsellor first. If the change still seems necessary, look for a natural break — the school holidays, the end of a school year — to make the change. Then follow the 'changing school' procedures set out later in this chapter.

Choosing a school checklist

Look for some of these features, but don't expect all of them! If you score on more than half then you've found a good school:

- Preschool children are invited to at least one orientation day before starting
- A school introductory brochure is available for new parents
- The school is close to home and/or is easily accessible
- Your child's friends from preschool and/or the neighbourhood are also starting at the local school
- Other kids in the family have done well and enjoyed the school
- Students look reasonably happy going into the school (and even

better, they look reasonably happy coming out!)

- School entrances are busy, chatty places
- Most kids wear the school uniform where uniforms are a school rule
- The school has an active clothing pool
- The school has taken steps to help the kids avoid skin cancer, such as prescribing wide-brimmed hats in summer, or has plenty of shade areas
- The children at play look busy and happy, and the teachers on playground duty seem interested and involved with them
- Teachers' cars are in the carpark well before the start of school
- School secretaries are warm, friendly and helpful people
- The school has a clear welfare or pastoral care policy (see also suggestions under 'Transition to middle or high school' in Chapter 5)
- There are regular parent–teacher nights
- Parents are involved in school affairs
- The school rules are simple, clearly stated, positive and well enforced
- You've heard good things about the school
- The principal and teachers seem keen to meet parents and involve them in school activities
- There is opportunity for the children eventually to join special after-school or lunchtime groups or activities such as music groups, sporting teams, debating teams and environmental clubs
- The school has a reputation for excelling in some particular area
- Reports of the school's success appear in the local media
- The school grounds are well presented and clean
- Playground equipment looks plentiful and in good shape

- The library is well stocked, open and inviting
- There are lots of resources like computers and musical instruments
- The school canteen is clean, sells mostly healthy food and the helpers are friendly
- There are special provisions for children with physical or learning difficulties
- The buildings are in good repair even if not modern
- Classrooms are generally attractive and busy with activity and colour
- Positive comments are heard coming from the classroom
- The teachers' morale appears good
- Kids and teachers greet each other both in and out of school
- The staff look after their appearance

Choosing a good school requires a broad, sensible judgment, taking account of many factors — not just lopsided opinion.

CASE STUDY
Andrea

Mr and Mrs Newton had separated but they didn't want that to affect their daughter's education. So they took her with them to several private and public schools. After those visits, they asked her which one she thought would be best for her education. She chose one they least liked. When they asked why she had chosen that particular school she said that she really liked the food smells coming from the canteen they passed on the way to the office. Sometimes I think we ask children to make decisions on things way beyond their scope or experience.

Public or private?

For some families few choices carry more significance or symbolism than the selection of public or private schooling for their children. While enrolments in both sectors are continuing to rise, private school education is gaining in popularity — maybe because parents think they can have more say in their kids' education, maybe because particular private schools have beliefs or values that parents feel are important, maybe because families have more disposable income and fewer kids to educate. Of course, for many families the issue is clear-cut because of their philosophy on education, their family's financial circumstances or religious commitments.

One of the most common mistakes is for parents to opt for some prestigious school because of its reputation as a caring school or as a high-achieving school, and to take little account of its expectations (e.g. religious), its policies, resources, facilities, curriculum, standards or electives. As a result, the whole family ends up feeling like square pegs in round holes.

One strong suggestion is that parents write down a shopping list of the important features of their educational requirements and beliefs. This will clarify what you really want for your child.

If you are unsure as to which way to go, here are some guidelines:

'Which school?' checklist

Generally, the socioeconomic mix of the school may be an indicator of academic performance, but actually there is little comparative information about the performance of schools. Obviously selective schools do well, and, just as obviously, there are good and bad public and private schools.

- Don't just accept promotional material; check the following:
  - What is the school's performance in basic skills tests or external exams compared to the state average?
  - What is the absentee rate of students?
  - If trying to choose between public and private what's the

15

retention rate into the senior years, and how many subjects are offered, particularly electives?

- ■ What are the school's discipline, homework and assessment policies?

If the school is unwilling to disclose these there may be cause for concern.

- Any religious or other family moral commitments must rank high in the decision-making process as school is meant to be an extension of, not in competition with, a family's values.

- Finance can be a big issue and you should remember that being able to afford to send a child to private school is not just a matter of paying the fees — it also involves affording the 'extras' where costs tend to mirror the fees; that is, the higher the fees, the higher the extras. As a rule of thumb I suggest you budget on twice the school fees.

- It is preferable to get the best possible match between your values and your child's interests and abilities, on the one hand, with the school's staffing, style, resources and curriculum on the other. At primary levels it's possible to mould these somewhat through your selection of the school, but at high school much more weight needs to be given to the match between school electives and your child's preferences.

- By far the most important considerations are the practical ones such as transport, uniforms, friendships and, if you choose a private school, such basic issues as whether you can afford to do the same thing for your other kids.

CASE STUDY
Robert

John was a prominent member of the old boy network of the private school he had attended. Understandably, he was keen for Robert to follow in his footsteps so, at age 6, Robert left the family farm every day for the town's private prep school. The school was very large and social, and had a very welfare-orientated philosophy. Robert was soon identified as a 'loner' who was teased by some of the tougher kids. The staff worked hard to help Robert but over several years his inability to mix and fit in became more pronounced despite all efforts. When Robert began refusing to go to school his father agreed, after a lot of persuasion, to let Robert try the small, local public school. Robert, back on the land and near his mates, started to enjoy a new cosy environment that lifted his morale within days.

Tips from teachers

✍ 'I am a public schoolteacher with one child at public primary and one at private high school. The private school has been good for my son's sense of self-worth because no one picks on him for wanting to study and do well in his work. But my other son will probably stay in the public system because he's more sporty and wants to stay with his mates and is keen on the wider range of electives that the local high school has to offer. I suppose it all boils down to "horses for courses".'

Juggling work and school

It is a fact that the majority of the mothers and most of the fathers with primary- and high school-aged children are in the workforce. Many mothers are particularly sensitive about the impact of this work/career commitment on their children but if the situation is well handled the children need not be disadvantaged in any appreciable way. Research from the

17

Institute of Family Studies in Melbourne has shown that the self-esteem of both mother and children was generally enhanced by the return to work. But I'd like to add that wherever possible there are big family gains if that return to the workforce can be delayed by a year, or preferably two, to allow parent (not necessarily Mum) and child the time to really get to know and be comfortable with each other.

But it's not easy. There's the daily rush of getting up early to get the kids dressed and breakfasted, their hair done and teeth cleaned, organise the lunches, put the washing out, tidy the house and deposit the children in time to enjoy a good traffic snarl before a day's work. Then it's back home to take in the washing, cook dinner, clean up, handle the homework and iron out whoever or whatever has any wrinkles. No wonder the wheels fall off at weekends. Overworked parents can be overwound, overused and frequently out of time to relax and recover, and the very thing that the extra work was meant to provide, a happy family, disappears behind the mist of the materialism myth. It's not just mothers being found wanting either. In a large survey in 1999 (funded by the government's Men's Role in Parenting Project) of more than 1000 dads, the researchers found some sobering statistics: Dads spend an average of 47 hours at work — that's the equivalent of a 6-day week; 68 per cent said they were stressed by their workload and didn't get enough time with their kids; 33 per cent worked more than 50 hours a week.

In another study, little kids drew family pictures with Dad in close, but 9–12-year-olds drew fathers as more distant and surrounded by material goods such as boats and cars and surfboards. 'This spells danger,' says Professor Don Edgar, from Melbourne University's Centre for Workplace Cultural Change, as children's self-esteem is largely influenced by how often they see their dads. 'If a father's not there, it's like driving on two cylinders instead of four,' he adds.

Assuming, as is the case in 95 per cent of families, that mother is the domestic coordinator, here are a few survival hints.

What to do

Don't just expect your partner or kids to help — clarify what help you need, when and where, and then work out with the family who is best able to take over responsibility (not just 'helping' with many reminders along the way!).

Financial concerns can destroy marriages if they are allowed to become the first priority. Your family is your biggest investment. In fact, the cost of the first child to the family is, on average, in excess of $350 000 in terms of outlays and lost income. So it's worth getting it right!

If you must return to work early then try to organise one regular, warm, cosy, loving, special caretaker. Grandparents are often keen and eager but I caution against using them on a regular basis. In the long term it can cause resentment if they want a holiday or if they start to take over. Use grandparents as back-up or on special occasions, and check out council-run family day care for very young children — it's a nice, cosy, home-based alternative. Some parents, even at this age, prefer long day care. Certainly kindergartens, preschools, and long day care offer wonderful experiences for young children, especially once they reach the age of sociability (at approximately 2 years). Standards of care in Australian early childhood centres are among the best in the world and subsidies are readily available for low-income earners or parents with special needs. Probably the best source of good information on this topic is Rosemary Lever's book *Guide to Child Care in Australia*.

Keep plugging away for the job that will suit the family best. You may need to check out before or after school care but, to be honest, I don't like the idea of kids going to multiple carers in one day (before school, preschool, after school, etc.). While it might suit careers, I find some kids become very stressed and distressed and, as a result, become very difficult little customers when parents do take over. There are too many adjustments to be made to too many people. Kids need down time, lap time, cuddle time, play time … our time. To an exhausted ego there's no such thing as quality time.

If you have school-aged children and you can't be home before or with them (see 'Latchkey kids' on page 218), then make sure that the under-10s have some company. For the older ones who come home alone by choice, consider getting a pet to provide company, leave friendly messages around or phone from work. No one enjoys coming home to an empty house.

The big trap is failing to change gears between work and home. Some parents arrive home still in top gear and come on too fast; others are still thinking about work and can't add the kids' load to an overcrowded, overwound mind. To counter this, American psychologists suggest you do some 'decomposing' as follows:

- On your way home change mental gear — turn off work and go into limbo (music if you're driving, reading if you're on public transport, and don't get them mixed!).

- Before you hit the front door, project beyond that door to what might be happening on the other side (kids fighting, wanting homework help, kids competing to get your attention first, urgent dobbing and counter-dobbing to be done, etc.).

- Take the pace off and, if you can, have a few cosy routines or play your favourite CD for the first few minutes home.

- Don't touch the phone, the answering machine, the computer or the mail for the first half hour.

- Give yourself 5 minutes 'unwinding' time.

But kids haven't changed; most still prefer to come home to an occupied house. If you've decided to stay home to look after Australia's greatest assets, the children, then it's just as important that life retains its vitality or the four walls will feel like padded ones. Remember, you are home for the sake of the family, not to be a servant to the kids. Martyrs don't make good mothers or fathers, so share the work around whether you are working inside, outside or probably both.

CASE STUDY

Stevie

One of the saddest cases we've worked on involved a boy from a prominent local family, who was placed in a detention centre at the age of 12. Stevie looked up to his father almost as if he were a god. The irony of this was that Stevie's dad was somewhat of a god, a vision that passed fleetingly in and out of Stevie's life but never really touched him. In therapy Stevie's father was adamant that he was an excellent provider. There was no doubt about this: Stevie had the latest baseball jacket and top-of-the-range running shoes. Stevie's mum tried her best, but the boy was a bit like his dad, born on the go and with a will of his own.

Unfortunately he was somewhat too strong for his mother to handle on her own. The combination of a difficult child and a busy father was a disaster. Dad had made good his promise that his kids would never be without in the way he had been as a child. Only the emotional care and stability Stevie required as a difficult child was never provided. As some sage said, our kids would be much richer if we spent half as much money on them and twice as much time.

Tips from teachers

✍ 'It's sad to see so many parents in such a hurry that they show no interest in what their child may have made or done during the day. Often we see their children just so excited to show them their art and Mum will say "Mm, lovely," then put it in the bin on the way out. In time I believe those children won't want to produce their best or be proud of their work and then parents will complain that their kids are lazy and don't try.'

Changing schools

In an interesting article in the *Financial Review*, much to the surprise of the editor, I gather, more than 50 per cent of fathers surveyed reported that they would knock back a promotion if it meant the family had to be dislocated and the kids had to change school. But for many 'successful' families, career progress often means some relocation. On the children's stress inventory, moving home and losing friends ranks as high as divorce or the loss of a job on their parents' stress scale. On the positive side, as for any stress, a caring, loving and well-prepared family will experience little trauma, unless teenagers are involved!

For most kids, moving causes a sense of loss, which can be alleviated by some honest open family talk and adjustment. Don't be frightened to let them know that you feel a bit of sadness, too. For many kids fear of the unknown is the worst because their imaginations work overtime. It will really dispel their fears if you can visit the new town and put the 'boogie monster' to rest by showing them the realities rather than the fantasies, especially if they can check out McDonald's, Hungry Jack's and other sacred sites. But probably the most important contact to make when the kids take an orientation trip to the new town is with other kids who will be going to the same school, preferably those in the same class and of the same sex. That way they know they won't be facing a brave new world totally alone. Many schools also have a buddy system or peer support program to help new kids settle. Here are a few other do's and don'ts to soften the landing.

DO

✓ Do make at least one visit to the new area before moving. While you are there get hold of a map and see if your kids can find out where the swimming pool is, where Dad or Mum will work, where the video library is, and so on.

✓ Do find the local park and unwind there a bit to let them know they have landed somewhere nice.

✓ **Do** check out the availability of the clubs, sports or hobbies your children are interested in. Perhaps you could also organise contacts with adults and kids, to be taken up when you arrive.

✓ **Do** buy the kids special little address books to jot down new names and numbers and, more importantly, to record the addresses and numbers of the friends they are leaving behind so that they know they can still make contact.

✓ **Do** let them take old mementoes and farewell presents; even if you think they are rubbish, they do give a sense of security.

✓ **Do** investigate the new school well before the family is due to move; look at starting and finishing times, holiday dates, special curricula or sports, electives (if high schools are involved), uniforms, what books are needed, how books are to be covered, bus timetables, where the children can get their lunches, school bag fashions, their teachers' names, whether any excursions have been planned — anything that will help your kids feel well prepared.

✓ **Do** if at all possible, try to move at the end of a year or during school holidays. Many families arrange for one parent to go on ahead to sort out where the family will live and generally get settled so it's an easier transition.

✓ **Do** be sensitive to the kids' feelings. For single parents who have to move or for families that are splitting up, the trauma of a new school, a new home and no friends is trebled. It's vital that these kids be given latitude to stay in touch, take photos and so on, even more than for the average home mover. Maybe, if time, house and fences suit, buy a little pet the kids can become attached to; this may ease the pain and loneliness considerably. Once the children have arrived, for their sanity and survival link them up with clubs, teams or other kids as fast as possible.

✓ **Do** give the new school as much information as you feel comfortable disclosing, so they have an understanding of where the child is coming from and can make the best possible adjustments and placement.

✓ **Do** explain to your kids that everything they own goes with them — some little kids think you leave it all behind.

DON'T

✗ **Don't** try to oversell the move or the lonely reality will hit the kids even harder.

✗ **Don't** hide the upcoming move from them; it's worse if a friend tells them the 'good news' that they are moving out.

✗ **Don't** tell them they have just got to be tough; compassion breeds security.

✗ **Don't** be too pushy — give the kids time to assimilate.

✗ **Don't** change schools just because the kids want to escape the one they're at for some reason — can't do the work, bullying, no friends, etc. Running away from a problem is rarely the answer; solving the problems where they are is much more likely to build self-confidence. On the other hand, if they're older and they're dead-set keen not to run away from problems, but to go to another school for some positive reason, often this kind of move does work out because they have made the commitment to make it work.

CASE STUDY
Jared

Jared let everyone know he was at school from day one. The staff certainly knew everything Jared did because he stood out like a sore thumb as the most difficult child in a small school population. 'Jared' was the not-so-nice name on every teacher's lips. As so often is the case with disruptive and attention-seeking kids, there was family friction at home and eventually his parents split up. Jared's mum moved back to her parents' house and Grandpa, who was financially comfortable, paid for Jared to go to a private school. With less home friction, no reputation to live down, a firm but friendly granddad around, lots of other kids to mix with and a school where his new teachers dealt differently with his behaviour, Jared began to settle down and work. He says he feels good now so he acts good.

Tips from teachers

✍ There was an overwhelming consensus among teachers surveyed that you don't change schools just because kids want to. The issue should be discussed with the school first to see what it is that the kid isn't coping with. If the child has interests that don't suit the norm, there may be children in other grades who do have similar interests whom they could meet.

Chapter 2

Getting to School

M ost of us can remember having trouble getting to school at some time during our 10 to 12 years there, but for many children it's not just hard, it's impossible. This chapter looks at ways to overcome such problems as kids who can't leave home, can't get to school, can't get ready on time, are forever losing things or can't organise themselves, or are forever 'sick' on school days. Some of the statistics on school absenteeism you may find quite alarming.

Separation anxiety

Normally separation anxiety is linked with young babies who, at about the age of 9 months, are mature enough to remember who's who and who's not. They might explore away from Mum for a few seconds, but they always check to make sure she's still there. Gradually, with time, with confidence and as other people develop a growing place in their lives, the anxiety settles down until in adult life it might only provoke a few pangs at Christmas and on Mother's Day. If, however, there has been some trauma that threatens their confidence, such as a stay in hospital, or an illness, if mother is overly anxious or dependant on the child, or if the kid is just naturally anxious and insecure, then the battle can last much longer.

For these anxious kids the transition to preschool or school, or any real separation from Mum, can become very threatening. It has nothing to do with loving their mother more than other kids do, although a lot of parents mistakenly believe this because it's nice to be needed. Over time these symbiotic attachments can become very bitter as both parent and child are deprived of life away from each other and are caught in what we term a conflict–dependency bind. Here are a few ideas to prevent that overpowering anxiety.

How to help
- Make sure your children have plenty of contact with other adults so they learn to feel more confident with others. Try to get your partner, family or friends to take the kids to school and/or out somewhere so they don't become over-dependent.
- Build up little steps of independence so your child feels he or she is growing big and strong. This might start with the child playing near Mum but not with her, on a one-to-one basis. The next steps might be coping with playgroup, then staying with other kids and adults while Mum does some shopping or visits the doctor. Finally the child might stay with Grandma or another close relative or friend while Mum and Dad go out.
- Never sneak away from your children. Make the first separations brief so they become confident you'll come back.
- Some parents leave something personal behind to give an added sense of security.
- Make sure your child knows what to do in case you are late (where to sit, who to sit with, etc.).
- If the kids are worried about how sad you will be without them while they are at school, tell them what you'll be doing at, for example, recess, lunch or sports time, so they know you are okay. Just don't make it sound too attractive!
- If you find you are relying too much on your kids to

27

make up for a loss of love on other fronts (for example, through death or separation), then it's probably best to get some counselling for yourself so you learn to lean on someone your own size. Many clingy kids reflect turmoil on the domestic front that has made them feel anxious and insecure.

- Link the kids up to peer groups in teams or hobbies so that they will gain satisfaction from mingling with the mob.

- The best way to help anxiety is by showing or instilling confidence — if your kids sense you are feeling okay about yourself and about them, then they will feel okay. Be positive about the school, the teacher and the other children.

CASE STUDY
Belinda

Belinda looked like any healthy happy 10-year-old. She had lots of friends, loved horses, origami and calligraphy, and she had one of those faces that lit up when she smiled. But she wasn't smiling any more. Every time she left home it tore her insides out. She went to camp and teachers said she just sobbed inconsolably. She went to school and couldn't cope.

Belinda had every reason to develop separation anxiety. Her younger brother had died two years earlier and her mother was so devastated that they had moved house and changed schools. Her mother still couldn't talk about anything personal without breaking down. I'd never met Belinda's father. His job as a marketing manager took him away from home quite a bit, but Belinda's mum told me that since Jamie's death he had buried himself in his work. When Belinda wanted to understand what was wrong I explained that when a family loses something or someone the rest of the family hangs on to each other more tightly for comfort and to make sure no one else will get lost.

Sometimes their grip on each other is so tight that when any of them leaves the family circle they really feel the wrench.

We arranged special counselling for Mum so she could start to work her grief out and let life back in. Then Belinda, Mum and I decided that Belinda could go to school with her best friend so she wouldn't feel the wrench as much when she left her mother. We also arranged for Belinda and her group of friends to do some urgent stapling and office work at school at lunchtime so she wouldn't have time to feel alone and miss her mother. So far so good. Belinda and Mum are both keeping notes about new frontiers forged, new independence won and also about what's helping them along the way.

Tips from teachers

✍ 'I've always told mothers of anxious kids to leave something behind so the kids will know Mum will be back. One mother told her child she could take something from her bag to reassure her, so the child grabbed a tampon and raced around the room with it, much to the mirth of staff and the embarrassment of Mum.' The consensus of teachers on this question was to reassure parents that the kids will be okay, and just to say goodbye quickly and go.

School sickness and absenteeism

Absenteeism from school is a major problem. About 10 per cent of students are absent each day, and that's the average. When you realise that some children never miss a day, this figure means that others are absent from school dangerously often. Not only does frequent absence mean that kids won't reach their potential and will drop in academic confidence, but it can also drop their social confidence if they aren't at school to nourish their friendships.

What's more, we have become increasingly aware of how vulnerable young people can be to exploitation by adults for drugs, alcohol, smoking or involvement in pedophile activity. There can usually be little argument that during the school day the safest place for a child is at school! Students of all ages are less likely to become victims or perpetrators of crime if they are at school. Parents play a key role in the attitudes children develop towards school attendance. Research has found five factors behind poor attendance:

- Family background — poverty, disinterested parents, criminal activity, broken homes, parent absence, many siblings, etc.
- Academic difficulties — special needs not recognised or catered for, language problems, etc.
- Relationship problems — personality clash with teacher, bullied, bullying and unpopular, misfit in class, social difficulties, separation anxiety from parent, precocious or unable to relate to peers, etc.
- Behavioural difficulties — reaction to home problems, hyperactivity, school phobia, anxiety, psychiatric problems, aggressiveness/stubbornness, etc.
- School-based problems — ineffective monitoring, poor welfare system, poor home — school liaison, lack of relevance of the curriculum, unawareness by staff of student need, etc.

Of the 10 per cent away each day it's estimated that 1–2 per cent are absent for a legitimate reason other than illness (e.g. family funeral, family commitment), 4 per cent are absent due to illness — which leaves approximately 4 per cent of students still absent. Education authorities' research indicates that truancy (defined as students being absent without parental knowledge) is less than half of 1 per cent.

This means that, on average, at least one child in every primary class is away each day with what is termed 'parent-condoned absenteeism'. This situation is seen by education authorities and police as a major problem.

The best way to prevent major attendance problems is to have a home policy that if it's a school day and the kids are not sick, they go to school.

Of course the problem for many parents is to know whether the kids are really sick or not. Head and tummy ailments are clear favourites, but some of the more creative ones include being unable to stand, blurred vision, the recurrence of an earache 'only worser', red biro-looking spots on the tummy, and writer's cramp. One child even claimed premonition of a bomb threat. Parent explanations can be just as comical — 'she's got a cartridge in her knee', 'he suffers from a genital bad back', 'she had to go back to the doctor's for her leg', 'she hates going and has become an electric newt [elective mute]', 'his father was home', 'couldn't wake the bugger', 'please excuse my child as she was absent'.

If your child often feels sick before school, or if the recovery rate after 9 a.m. is remarkable, it's worth looking for outside causes such as too many late nights, too much junk food, or just too much else on. Maybe taking sickies is a family virus, or perhaps the child is failing in the playground or in the classroom. An ounce of prevention is worth a pound of cure, so try a balanced diet, a balanced life, some time to talk about any problems and a general drop in home bustle and bristle. If a happier, problem-free home doesn't help, then talk to the teacher or counsellor and get some school or remedial help — and then keep talking until you are satisfied that help is happening/forthcoming. A day at home is rarely the cure.

'Sickness' checklist

- Is there a medical reason?
- Does the sickness happen every morning or just on school days?
- Does the child get miraculously better by about 9 a.m.?
- Has the teacher indicated that the child was ill at school?
- Does the sickness happen at special times, for example, when the child gets up or gets dressed?
- Are there more tears than are normally associated with an illness?
- Is there more anger than sadness if the child is forced to go to school?
- Does it seem to make a difference who takes the child to school?
- Are there other emotional indicators that it's 'school sickness', such as more nightmares, a loss of energy, the child becoming clingy, etc.?

DON'T

✗ **Don't** make appointments for the child with hairdresser, etc. during school hours if your child has a chequered school attendance history.

✗ **Don't** allow kids to stay home on sport days — in fact sport is an important part of a child's development.

Maybe you need to find the type of sport that suits their build, talents, preferences and personality.

✘ **Don't** give your kids a day off just in case they're sick — instead, give the school a phone contact number if needed.

✘ **Don't** allow them to run around and have free time — if they're sick they should be in bed.

✘ **Don't** make the time off special in any way: no computer, no TV, no friends after school, no special lunches.

✘ **Don't** take your child shopping on a school day even if the shopping centre is marketing kids' specials.

✘ **Don't** allow them out of the house even after school — if they're too sick for school, then they're too sick for play.

✘ **Don't** take holidays during term if possible (especially if the kids have a history of school aversion) as it makes attendance harder on their return.

✘ **Don't** deny the possibility of a school problem; make a fairly fast appointment to talk to the teacher.

✘ **Don't** deny the fear — it's real — but if it's not easing get professional help from a counsellor or psychologist.

Problems	Helpful hints	Advantages
Won't get out of bed	Set specific time to be out of bed	Routine becomes easier
Won't go to bed	Set specific time to go to bed	Peace and quiet for parent, rest for kids
Can't find school clothes	Have them ready the night before	No excuses/no panic
Dawdles over breakfast	Set time to start and finish	Less mess/no fights

33

Problems	Helpful hints	Advantages
Long hair not styled	Select simple style that can be easily done	Child can do own hair
Can't find school books	Have them ready the night before	Child responsible/less hassle
Homework not done	Set specific time for homework	Homework completed
Too much TV watching	Watch only specific programs	Other jobs completed
Fighting with brothers/ sisters	Stay calm, have them concentrate on their jobs	Children learn respect for each other
Chores not finished	Finish them after school	Children know what is expected
School bag missing	Have ready night before/use substitute	Children learn to look after things
School lunches not ready	Make night before/ go without	Children soon learn
Mum's shopping day	Be firm, children go to school	School routine reinforced
School test day	Be firm but let teacher know of exam nerves	The child's needs can be addressed
School sports day	Sport's good for body and brain	Healthier and brighter kids
Child's birthday	Be firm, birthdays aren't holidays	School routine reinforced

CASE STUDY
Emma

Emotional Emma was a world champion at suffering school sickness. She had settled very well into school in her first year but had some unfortunate experiences at the end of her second year at primary school. In the last few weeks of the school year Emma developed a middle ear infection and needed several days' recuperation. Her mother then let her have the last five days of the year off as she had had such a stressful time. Little wonder that Emma soon learnt how to become 'sick' to perfection.

By the time we saw Emma she was throwing up before school and also on the way. Medical checks revealed no illness other than stress. We talked about whether being sick was much fun. Then we separated the need to be sick from Emma and made it into a sick monster that she was going to get rid of. We drew the monster, then put 'sick spots' all over it. The aim was that Emma would make the sick monster sick by going to school. Every day she beat him she would put on another 'sick sticker'. Emma's mum also needed a little help with her own separation problems and phobias, and we suggested ways to change the routine in the morning. We also concentrated on talking about only the good things about school and gave the monster an extra spot for each. Within three weeks and with the help at home and from a very supportive teacher, Emma was a healthy attender with a very sick monster covered in spots stashed away in Mum's scrapbook.

Tips from teachers

✍ The general consensus among teachers is that if you think the kids are malingering, send them to school — teachers can call you if they're really sick.

✍ 'Give school-sick children a dose of some not so nice tonic — it's good for them and will soon sort out the sick from the pseudo-sick.'

School phobia

School phobia is a special case of 'school sickness'. It's not just a fear of going to school — it makes attendance a downright impossibility. There are other important differences, too: for example, there may be no physical complaints (although nausea, headaches and tummy-aches are nearly always present), and generally school phobia is more a fear of leaving home than a fear of going to school. The other big difference is in degree. Usually kids with school fear can be coaxed along or offered an incentive to get them under way: their resistance is frequently more symbolic than real. With children suffering from school phobia the fear is quite frantic, the chances of coaxing them on their way are slim, their failure to meet solutions is frustrating, and their resistance to school is extreme to the point of being dangerous.

The reasons such a phobia develops are many and varied. In every case I've seen the kids have been worriers who swallow their anxieties. But as about half the population (including adults!) can be classified as 'internalisers', that on its own is not a sufficient explanation. Frequently a child with school phobia may have experienced some trauma associated with going to school or leaving home. Learning difficulties, however, are rarely the cause, as the majority seems to be of at least average intelligence. The trauma triggers I've come across include a parent disappearing from the family while the child was at school; something nasty happening to them on the way to school; being assaulted or hounded by a bully at school; soiling or wetting their pants at school; parents splitting up or arguing a lot; a mother who is depressed and upset; some form of suicidal talk within the family ranks; and a death in the family.

Children with school phobia are at real risk and need quick, clever and professional help.

How to help

- Share the problem with the school and be honest and open about what is happening.
- Don't expect logical, rational means to sort the problem out — school phobia is not a rational problem. Children can promise the world and say they'll go the next day and mean it, but when they are faced with the reality their head is no match for their heart. They might know their terror is silly, but they can't do a thing about it. Worse still, if they have managed to avoid the problem before by blaming something else or by feigning sickness, then guess what will happen next time.
- Don't just tell school-phobic kids how to beat their phobia — let them see and feel success. This means helping them reach very small goals at first, so small that they almost stumble over success without trying. Small goals may be something as elementary as walking past the school, getting dressed in their uniform or just walking down the street. It's important to start small and build from there.
- Don't let your kids' fears or their capacity to make you feel to blame push you into a corner, bending over backwards to make them happy, when the real problem is that they are sinking fast and are using excuses to hide their fear. There's an old saying that if you bend over backwards for your kids you are bound to lose your balance.
- The other side of the coin is that any stay at home on

37

school days, if you can't get them there, has to be as uninteresting as possible so that time off from school isn't attractive. This means no television, eating playlunch and lunch at the same time as they would at school, no snacks, no computer time and, if Mum had plans to go out, that's what she does, providing arrangements have been made for someone to keep an eye on things back home.

- In almost every case, if you are faced with an absolute refusal to go to school or with typical sweaty, panicky behaviour, then the school counsellor (or private child psychologist), home–school liaison officer (if there is one) and maybe even the family doctor should be consulted. Whatever you do, don't try hitting phobic kids out of their 'silly' behaviour.

CASE STUDY
Angela

Angela was a bright and high-spirited 9-year-old who excelled at school. Mum was an artist and since her separation had been away from home more than she would have liked, to do business, exhibit her work, etc. Angela started to get mystery illnesses that kept her home from school. At first a guilt-ridden mum dropped everything and tried to stay home with her until she was better but doctors could never find any real cause, despite the school day-consuming and exhaustive tests that were undertaken. Mum started to realise that it was all in Angela's mind so she tried forcing her to school. Angela would hold on to the car seat belt or the door, pull Mum's hair and scream if anyone tried to force her out of the car. In fact, on several occasions she tried to jump out of the moving car on its way to school.

Mum's business was going backwards in a hurry while she was trapped at home, and so was Angela. They tried the soft-shoe approach, driving past the school, going to school in after-school hours, having Angela's friends call in to take her, but nothing worked, not even anti-anxiety medication, hypnosis, teacher visits, etc.

Angela got on well with Mum's sister so we ended up telling Mum to take her to Aunty's place, leave her there, get on with her business, come back there for bed and breakfast and then take off for work the next day. We did this for just 3 days. Angela found she could survive without Mum but she missed her friends. Mum returned home, took a hard line with Angela about getting to school and hasn't had any trouble since. Sometimes, the more severe the problem, the more firm the cure needs to be.

Tips from teachers

✐ The general consensus of teachers surveyed was that teacher, counsellor and home must work together on problems of school resistance.

School-slow kids — the dawdlers

Think of the best dawdler you know and spare a moment's silence for the demented parents. Some dawdlers are like the absent-minded professor, some are confused, others are unwell or have weak 'engines', some just enjoy idling, others have overactive brakes, and still others are trying to put the brakes on overactive parents. Many dawdlers, however, are just coasting in first gear, waiting for a parent to take over. Whatever the reason, dawdlers are guaranteed to produce high levels of domestic stress.

How to help
- Your first check should be a home check. Are the kids just overtired and over-exhausted — too much else on, staying up too late, non-stop pace, etc.?
- Your second action should be a full medical check. There can be a hundred important medical reasons for dawdling, including blood disorders, heart disorders, infections and even some mild forms of epilepsy.
- Your third line of action should be a psychological check. If you get the medical all-clear then it could be that the dawdling is a symptom of depression, of fear, of low self-esteem, or of an inability to make choices or decisions. Fear of being wrong or of being laughed at can put children under so much pressure that their inactivity becomes like the calm eye of the cyclone.
- If your child is basically happy, however, and if the tests show nothing is wrong and the school says they are coping pretty well, then check your management style. If you are a whirlwind that fusses and fumes and fixes and finishes the kid's fumbles, then the child can become a family 'passenger' waiting for your next adrenalin wave to carry them through. So treat the problem as a case of bad teaching on your part and make some changes. Set a few tasks to be done on time, withhold favourites like TV or breakfast until basic

chores are done, and let the child know that you've made the big decision to let them start running their own life. Learn to accept any failures early on and encourage any small successes in self-management until the child is in good shape.

- If the situation is not improving or if your child is resisting, then ask how they think the problem can be beaten. A nice quiet chat in place of a favourite TV show should get the message across that you mean business.
- But remember that there is a better than even chance that your child is reacting to a hectic home. It's almost as if they have noticed how time pressures have destroyed your sanity and is determined not to do likewise.
- If you've been reminding your kids to hurry for years, it would be fair to suggest that reminders are not working. Try it this way: get their attention first, make eye contact, tell them once what you want done, ask them to repeat it (or, even better, give a choice so their mind is totally on the task), then check your success. But your style must be one of practice, not preaching.

CASE STUDY
Warren

Warren was a classic case. He would arrive at school every day looking quite the neatest kid in his class, but his mother was paying a high price in sanity to make this happen. Every school day was the same: a dozen calls to get him out of bed, a dozen more to get him out of his pyjamas and to turn off the television. Then a dozen hurry-ups to get him through his breakfast while he contemplated how long it took a Weet-bix to soak up a cup of milk. Eventually his mum would have to dress him herself, brush his hair and drive him to school because he always missed his bus.

Warren wasn't really worried. He always got to school,

didn't he? His mother realised that Warren was the puppeteer in the morning drama and that she was growing old fast while he stayed young and irresponsible. So we developed a plan which Mum felt she could act upon.

Warren would be woken up once only. If he needed a second call that would suggest overtiredness and he would go to bed 15 minutes earlier that night. There was to be no television before school. There was to be no breakfast until he was dressed and his bag was packed. Warren would be taken to school at the due time regardless of his state of readiness (breakfasted or not).

The arrangements were discussed with Warren and formally agreed upon. All the tasks to be completed before school were listed, as were the consequences of cooperation or non-cooperation.

Warren has only been driven to school once in his pyjamas and is quickly learning to manage himself well.

Tips from teachers

✍ Turn off the TV, set clear time limits with rewards for improvement and let the child miss out on a few things so they become more motivated to hurry themselves up.

Disorganised and forgetful kids

Disorganised and forgetful kids have to rank as the most frustrating characters on Earth. Most are lovely children — you want to have a good relationship with them and a peaceful life at home — but they keep wrecking your plans for domestic sanity with a room that looks like a bomb has hit it and constant cries of 'Mum, where's my ... ?' or 'Who took my ... ?'

Some are born that way, others copy the behaviour of family members, and still others are allowed to stay that way thanks to 'loving' parents who do the thinking, remembering and organising for them.

Some kids, often those who are good talkers but rather absent-minded, are hopeless with their eyes. They honestly have a lot of trouble retaining mental pictures of where things are and where they go. By contrast, children who do retain mental pictures more easily (often tidy and well-organised kids who know how things should look) have a much clearer imprint to call upon.

Other forgetful kids are so preoccupied with one all-consuming idea or problem that it takes up all their mental energies, leaving nothing over for day-to-day trivia such as where they put their bag or that note from the teacher. The consuming problem could be to do with friends or family, or even insecurity about their own self-image, but whatever the source the effect is similar: they just can't keep their mind on what they are doing.

However, forgetfulness can also be a symptom of two other problems discussed in the next chapter: epilepsy and/or Attention Deficit Hyperactivity Disorder. In the former there is a kind of epilepsy which used to be called 'petit mal', but more often now is called 'partial epilepsy' or 'absences'. In this, the child may be given an instruction but loses it due to a brief electrical brain switch-off. With Attention Deficit Hyperactivity Disorder the brain doesn't switch off, it just switches track. As the message reaches a connection point (synaptic gap), the message gets lost or weakened so other, more powerful, more visual information jumps in (i.e. they get distracted). It's worse at school because much of the information is in word form, it's abstract, it's not there, so it's easily lost. But put them in front of a TV or computer, where the information is fast, visible and stimulating, and they can be kept occupied for hours. There's the problem for schools! It's not the teacher's fault!

Here are a few ways to tell whether your child does have an internal problem or whether the forgetfulness and lack of organisation is externally inspired.

Organising checklist

- If your child is quite organised in sport, hobby or school work, but not at home, then the chances are that over-organising parents could be the problem.

- If the problem seems to be more a lack of responsibility in everything rather than an inability to get organised, then the chances are that the problem is over-protection.

- If they can remember things they have heard but can't remember things they've seen (where things go, where to put things, etc.), then the chances are that spatial skills may be a bit weak, making them appear disorganised. To cope adequately, such kids need to be more organised and have set spots to put things, with consistent insistence that items be returned where they belong.

- If the disorganisation stems from owning too many things, from overcrowding or hoarding, then the chances are that a few rules are needed, and maybe a halfway house (such as an attic, a shed or even a box) between belongings and the bin.

- If they're always in tears, uptight, over-reacting or emotionally exhausted, then the chances are that the disorganisation reflects a life in emotional chaos; low organisational skills may well reflect low self-esteem and an inability to plan effectively. To work this out just see whether they're much tidier or house-proud or organised after a friend's phone call or a good day at school.

- If they're forgetful, the first thing to do is to get a full medical check to exclude any physical, chemical or even neurological problems. If your child receives the all-clear, then ask a psychologist to investigate whether there are any personal, social or intellectual problems that are actively interfering with your child's concentration.

- If you want your child to learn to be more organised and remember better, then it will take some teaching:

  - Work out together set spots for their things to go.

- Insist kindly that things go back where they came from.

- Encourage their efforts to put their own things away — with your help if they're young.

- Plan a regular tidying-up time so they can rediscover things they've forgotten.

- Never find things for them ... with them, perhaps ...

- If your child is an 'absent-minded professor' they may need to carry a notebook in which to write messages to themselves or to have a fixed routine so that the day-to-day 'trivia' of life (e.g. emptying lunch boxes after school) becomes automatic. Or you could present the trivia as a challenge that they have to solve themselves, which will help it to become ingrained.

CASE STUDY
Mary

Mary was a popular child, but she never seemed to have the right equipment on the right day or the right book out at the right time and her school desk was described as a bomb site. Her teacher found her quite exasperating. Her homework was always late and rather messy. Her books were all dog-eared and her bag had everything in it but the kitchen sink. When we talked to Mary's mother we discovered that her bedroom was even worse!

After assessing Mary we found that the untidiness was more the result of the problem than the cause. Mary had a mild learning difficulty with order and sequence; she had trouble planning her time and knowing what followed what or how long things would take. Events in her daily life were, for her, just a jumble.

We decided that Mary's mum would make a checklist of things to be done each day before school and, as Mary loved breakfast, we made sure most were to be done before she ate. We also suggested that her mum run through the next day's events, putting them into sequence and explaining the arrangements when she went in to say goodnight to Mary.

Her mother and father also helped by setting up some clear rules and routines so Mary's mind could settle into a daily rhythm, minimising the possibility of 'order overload'. At school her teacher set up a diary, or what she called a 'chatter-book', in which she would outline Mary's homework, step-by-step at first, so Mary wouldn't become confused. As far as her bedroom went, the deal was that Mary couldn't go out to play on Saturday until it was tidy.

While the problem hasn't gone away, Mary now knows how to handle it. At last she is starting to put her life back in order.

Tips from teachers

✍ Use a diary/planner and make sure you're giving a good example of how to organise space or time yourself.

✍ 'My kids were okay on remembering things. But I've learnt a few tips from parents with forgetful kids. One stopped replacing things the second time they got lost and the kids had to do jobs and pay for lost items themselves from then on. Another parent said she cured it by getting out the Texta and warning her son that next time he lost something, she would put his name in large print on the outside of the item — she never had any more trouble.'

Chapter 3

In the Classroom

It's a funny thing, education. It was introduced to help children learn about life, but we take them out of life, put them behind four walls with little windows and big fences and proceed to tell them about life! That process may work well for the 'ear learners', those who are good at remembering, understanding and mentally manipulating words, but for the 'eye learners', the children who rely on seeing, holding and mentally manipulating images, or for the 'touch learners', those who are practical and good with their hands, the talk-and-tell regime can spell educational difficulty and an ego disaster.

This chapter looks at some of those classroom difficulties — not just in reading, 'riting and 'rithmetic, but also in spelling and important classroom attributes like memory, concentration, sequencing and thinking skills. The chapter also looks at problems that may affect a child's learning capacity, such as being underactive, hyperactive, slow, fast, worried or stressed.

But let me make one thing quite clear. Although these are in-classroom problems, the research is very clear that children learn best if home and school are in partnership. If home and school work together, children get a common and reassuring message. But, more than that, children's attitudes to schoolwork are born and bred at home. Trying hard, doing their best, handling mistakes, asking for help, enjoying learning, enjoying literature, cooperating with adults — these are all vital skills in the classroom but they're home-driven.

Reading problems

Remember that all preschoolers and young children have a reading difficulty— it takes time to get to know this crazy symbol system we call our written language. But by the age of about 7 or 8, most kids have sufficient neurological maturity and experience with the written word for us to be able to identify problems. In fact, some overseas school systems don't even try to teach kids to read until they're 8! This chart can help you discover whether your child may be developing, or already has, a reading problem. Follow these steps.

Reading difficulties checklist

1. Find a paragraph in a current school reading book.
2. Record about 3–5 minutes of your child reading into a tape recorder.
3. Supply any unknown words and encourage as you listen.
4. Do not correct errors unless they affect the sense of the paragraph.
5. Ask one or two questions to see what they've grasped.
6. Immediately write down your impressions, choosing, if possible, words from the behaviour column below.

Behaviour	Could it be	Action
Fidgety	Anxiety? Attention deficiency?	Confidence building/Help with concentration
Tearful	Anxiety? Manipulation?	Confidence building

Behaviour	Could it be	Action
Angry	Frustration? Embarrassment?	Consult the teacher and work together and/or organise tutor
Rubs eyes	Visual problems? An allergy?	See the eye doctor
Voice too soft	Scared of making errors?	Confidence building
Head held low	Poor posture? Visual problems?	Improve the seating/See the eye doctor
Reads slowly	Depression? Anxious about errors?	Try to make reading fun/Time –race read
Reads word by word	Low sight-vocabulary? Vision?	Work with fun sight cards/Give story outline first
Reads too fast	Attention deficiency? Has no interest? Too competitive?	Help with concentration Work on anxiety
Omits words	Poor concentration? Low phonic skills? Poor word attack?	Help with punctuation Practise for fluency/accuracy
Mixes words up	Visual problems? Anxiety? Poor word attack?	Confidence building/Have eyes checked
Mispronounces words	Speech problems? Anxiety?	Consult a speech pathologist/ Confidence building

Behaviour	Could it be	Action
Loses place	Anxiety? Visual problems?	Use finger pointing
Adds words	Inattention to detail?	Use finger pointing/ Practise oral reading
Repeats consistently	Poor concentration? Anxiety?	Help with concentration
Guesses	Trying too hard? Imaginative?	Give an incentive for attention to detail
Doesn't pause	Cannot follow meaning?	Use praise and incentives/ Practise for fluency/accuracy
Low comprehension	Words too hard? Ideas too hard?	Use cloze reading/ Discuss the meaning
Mumbles	Lack of confidence? Embarrassment?	Make reading fun/ Organise a tutor
Refusals	Poor word attack skills?	Use praise/Phonics
Grouped errors	Panic after first error? Lost meaning?	Practise oral reading

CONFIDENCE BUILDING Choose books that a child can read with 95+ per cent accuracy. This level will ensure good fluency and interest. Sessions should be no longer than 10–15 minutes. Praise should be easy and encouraging, not over the top, and should be for specific reading success.

SEATING Provide good lighting with no shadows; reinforce correct posture; ensure the chair and table are the correct height for the child.

EXPERIENCE Develop a good book-list; provide a reward for books read; introduce family reading or quiet time; allow reading before lights out; tape-record before and after reading practice; ask your child to read a story onto a cassette for a younger sibling; teach breathing at punctuation.

ORAL PRACTICE Read funny poems; let them ham up their reading; encourage a flowing rhythm and relaxed reading; pretend to read to an audience; ask them to read instead of wiping up; encourage them to read to little kids.

VOCABULARY Play games such as Scrabble, Boggle, Crosswords, Findaword; give them a new word book; teach dictionary skills.

FINGER POINTING It is okay to finger point as this supports the idea of one-to-one matching.

CLOZE Select a passage, then cover or white out every twentieth word, which the kids then have to guess. Gradually reduce to every tenth word. At first you can provide a random list of the missing words for the child to select from. As they gain confidence in this type of exercise you can fade out the support list.

CONCENTRATION See 'Concentration problems' (below).

ATTENTION DEFICIENCY A syndrome referred to later in this chapter and involving poor attention, poor impulse control and, sometimes, hyperactivity.

SIGHT WORDS Eighty per cent of everything we read contains sight words or very frequently used words. Schools can supply you with a list of sight words suitable for the level your child is at.

PHONEMIC AWARENESS The ability to listen to the sounds in words and blend words based on the sounds heard.

PHONICS The phonological process combines the knowledge of phonic letter–sound relationships and phonemic awareness or the ability to hear the sounds in the words.

WORD ATTACK SKILLS Children are taught to group sounds together in words from left to right and not just to guess at the word from the first one or two letters.

How to prevent reading problems

About 1 in 10 boys, 1 in 30 girls, and about 60 per cent of jail inmates, have a reading problem. So it's worth preventing the problem as much as possible. Every kid needs to be able to read, but how able they are will depend on how interested they are. Here are a few ideas to help.

- Start early — talking, singing, telling nursery rhymes and even pulling faces all build an interest in communicating.
- Show by reading whenever you can that you value reading.
- If you want the kids to read *for* you later on in life then the secret is first to let them read *with* you.
- Provide a variety of things that encourage reading — stories, comics, poems, plays, cartoons, reference books, recipe books.
- Toddlers particularly enjoy anything about babies or animals or the child's daily routine.
- For kids up to the age of 5 I still like the reading guide by Dorothy Butler called *Babies Need Books*, but your preschool, kindergarten or day care centre will be able to help with up-to-date information.
- Specifically for school-age children are the book clubs which make material available to schools; in fact, several large publishers and distributors have some form of age-graded reading guide.
- Make regular use of the local library as part of the family routine. Don't forget that your local librarian is trained to offer ideas, and that the library offers

serenity, space and peace of mind for frantic families.

- Tune in to *Sesame Street* or *Play School* and take note of the way they teach the kids — it's all about fun learning.
- Don't try teaching them phonics. If they are interested you can buy a wall frieze or make up a sound-book from old cards, but it must be fun, not homework.
- A major boon for reading has come with the Internet — kids now have an exciting reason to want to read and spell well so they can communicate to their mates via the chat lines or e-mail.

A good way to look at the challenge is to treat reading a book like riding a bike. Just think about it! When kids start riding we don't say, 'This is a pedal, say pedal' or 'This is how it starts a chain reaction. Hurry up, blend the parts.' We start by letting them have a go, by running alongside, by steadying them when they are shaky, picking them up when they fall and applauding every success. Well, so it should be with reading. Let them have a go — recognising pictures when they are 2, favourite signs like McDonald's and Hungry Jack's when they are 3, then a few survival words like 'Walk', 'Don't Walk', 'Exit', 'Enter', 'Do Not Disturb' or even one or two family names by the age of 4, until they begin having a go at copying or writing their own name.

The whole idea is that the more they enjoy it the more interested they will become. So read to them every day, show intense interest in their squiggles, talk and listen, record favourite stories on tape, build up their own book with pictures or photographs, give gift books, join a library ... in fact, anything that shows the kids that you treasure books. Once they are under way they'll want to know all about the parts — the phonics — so they can build new words. There are now many good books that kids find fascinating, but which are not too difficult. From today, start reading together — the pay-off is priceless. As the sign in our local bookshop says, 'Richer than I you never can be — I had a parent who read to me!'

How to help your kids improve their comprehension

- Look through the book before asking them to read it, discuss what you think it might be all about and get them to predict what they think will happen.
- During reading pause at times to get them to predict what might happen next, give them time to self-correct, but give them the words yourself if they have no success so that the flow of the story is maintained.
- After reading see if the kids can tell the story in their own words and in the right sequence by using prompts such as 'and then ...' .
- Some kids love drawing — have them draw the story sequence in comic or cartoon form.
- Have the kids extend the story beyond the printed end, or write a new ending, somewhat like the idea of the *Choose Your Own Adventure* books.
- Discuss the difficult words in the story before it's read — knowing what the hard words mean and how to say them has been shown to lift comprehension by 80 per cent!

How to handle reading problems

- If reading difficulties arise consult the support teacher for learning difficulties in your school or area and discuss the child's progress with the regular teacher too. There are now some excellent remedial programs around. The Spalding method appears to help children of all ages and makes good logical and phonetic sense. The Reading Recovery program has done wonders for young children showing early signs of reading difficulty, before they drop the bundle. And with children who are good 'right-brainers', that is, children who are good spatially, I've found the Reading for Sure program has produced some marvellous results. I'm sure there are other programs in your area that are just as good, it's just that I don't know them.
- For any child with reading problems it is a good idea to

have their eyes checked, but get a second opinion if glasses are to be prescribed or the kid is to undertake a program of optometrical exercises. While correctly prescribed glasses can work wonders for some struggling readers whose vision is the problem, I've personally not seen many kids improve reading just with eye exercises. The research I've seen says if you want your kids to read better, read to them and, most importantly, get them to read.

- Check for scotopic sensitivity. Professor Phillip Forman and his team at Newcastle University have evidence that some children have particularly sensitive eyes. Their eyes may well be in focus but they find the exercise of reading quite stressful. These children may complain of glare or of lines moving on the page or of some parts of the page being darker than others, or just generally tire of reading very quickly. If you suspect that this could be the problem, try the cellophane test first — get A4 pieces of cellophane in primary colours, place these one at a time on the page as the child is reading and see if they claim that any of those colours or any combination of colours makes the job easier. Such children may benefit from the coloured glasses sometimes referred to as Irlen lenses. Have a chat to your local eye doctor, mention the phrase 'scotopic sensitivity', and maybe the child will be referred for specialist assessment.

Tips from teachers

✎ The general consensus of teachers was that if parents wanted to have children enjoy reading then they should make sure to read plenty of stories to them.

✎ 'I was lucky enough to be at a lecture by Mem Fox, author of *Possum Magic* and other wonderful stories. She told the story of a mother who went up to the stage to thank a world-leading scientist for the wonderful lecture he had just given, and mentioned to him that she wanted her son to become a scientist too. She asked him what she could do to mentally prepare her son for this career, to which the scientist replied, "Read him a story". The mother laughed politely and asked, "But after I've read my son a story, what should I do then?" The scientist replied, "Read him another, and another". Nothing stimulates the mind of a child more than reading.'

Writing problems

You would be the exception if you believed that today's kids are better handwriters than kids in the pen-and-ink days. Years ago form, finish and pride in workmanship were almost as important as educational goals. Now education is expected to deal with a world that's creating and communicating information faster than ever before — and that requires speed and efficiency as never before. The goals have changed and the tools have changed. In the pen-and-ink days writing needed to be rounded and smooth to allow an even flow of ink on a nib. That in turn called for complex fine muscle control, which wasn't easy before the age of 8. With the invention of the ballpoint pen out went the pen and ink and out went the need to focus on form. Print has shifted from circles and verticals to ellipses and sloped strokes, while writing is made by the easiest possible linkage of these foundation forms. In a way how well you write is now no more important than how well you speak; what matters is that the communication is clear and fluent.

If kids enjoy writing and people enjoy what they are communicating, then the kids generally become good writers, but if their spelling is poor or their fine motor control is poor, then the kids receive praise rarely and tend to lose all enthusiasm for communicating in the written form.

If you want your children to be good writers, start early — don't leave it until they commence school. Encourage 2-year-olds by letting them experiment with a variety of implements on a variety of surfaces (walls excluded, of course). Some good combinations are: chalk on chalkboard; crayon, chubby chalk and Textas on paper; detergent foam on plastic; paint on plastic or paper; paint on gladwrap spread on the table; felt pens on paper; felt pens on whiteboards; fingers in sand; fingers in paint; and charcoal on newspaper.

From the age of 2 kids will produce some reasonable scribbles and circles, so praise all their efforts, just as you would real writing. Even the constipated little scribble-blobs that look like flies are special to them. As kids get older and start to read their own first name or write a cross or a letter as their signature, let them share in sending cards so their ego is in print. Try, if you can, to use printing when putting names on school clothes and equipment so they see the correct style early.

Encourage older kids to do lots of writing on cards,

shopping lists and letters. Let them use a wide variety of implements so that their writing keeps its freshness. Give them a container for their desk that can hold different types of pens and pencils so they can decorate their work and enjoy the end results. If your kids have a flair for good writing and enjoy producing attractive work, they might like to join the nearest calligraphy club.

How to help

- Don't force a young writer to stay in between lines.
- Encourage writing in every form that grabs their interest — ask the kids to help write the shopping list while you call out the items, send postcards to family and friends when on holidays, keep a diary of special events, write plays, make name tags and signs for things at home.
- Encourage your child to use a word processor or play games on screen using the mouse to form figures or letters.
- Display drawings and writing that your child has done at school.
- Play games such as Junior Pictionary.
- If your child is not a good writer, first make sure that it's not just lack of pride that a few of the ideas above might help.
- If their writing is too heavy or smeary, maybe a different pencil grade or pen point could make a difference.
- If the writing is jagged or does not stay within the lines, the chances are that there is a fine motor coordination problem; here an assessment by an occupational therapist would be a good idea.
- If you have a 'leftie', remember that writing from left to right is harder. With modern ballpoints these children can use the same grip as the right-handers, that is, pinching the pen between thumb and index finger and

resting it on the middle finger; but left-handers should have a multi-directional pen and hold it a bit further back so they can see what they are writing. The page should be left of centre, too, for easier access and better posture.

- If your kids are developing backaches or neckaches, then their chairs are either too low or too soft, or they are leaning too far over the page. Technically, the head should not be tilted too far forward, elbows should be level with the table, the seat should be firm, the feet comfortably on the floor and the non-writing arm should take the weight to allow the writing arm to glide over the writing surface.

- If you have tried everything for years and your high school child still doesn't write well, then maybe as soon as finances allow you should cut your losses and invest in a computer. These days there is a strong emphasis on children using computers to publish their writing at school with the consequence that there is less need for 'neat' handwriting. It also helps in the presentation of assignments and essays and prevents the unnecessary loss of marks because of untidiness or illegibility.

- If your child is writing with their head too close or at an angle to the page or with eyes partially shut, then make an appointment with an optometrist or ophthalmologist.

Writing problem checklist

Your child probably has a physical or expressive writing problem if they score 5 or more in a section of this checklist:

Letter formation
- Has difficulty tracing
- Has difficulty forming letters as well as others in their class do
- Has trouble writing on the line

- Holds pen or pencil awkwardly
- Uses excess pressure or effort in writing
- Switches hands when writing
- Has poor spacing between letters and words
- Writing always looks untidy
- Has very small or excessively large writing
- Has writing that can't be easily understood
- Body, head or paper position is awkward

Expressive writing
- Mixes up the order of words in sentences
- Stories lack any fluency or flow of thoughts
- Omits words — which shows that they are thinking faster than they are writing
- Doesn't like to or can't put thoughts into writing
- Begins a story but can't remember ideas
- Ignores punctuation
- Mixes story themes in one sentence
- Hates writing thoughts down
- Has poor vocabulary or performs better orally than in writing

How to help your children's writing improve
- If you are keen to improve your children's writing, then find the best piece of writing they've done and discuss it and encourage it in terms of:
  - neatness
  - even letter heights
  - well-made letters
  - placement on the line, not above or through
  - amount of crossing out
  - writing being the right size.
  - Photocopy this 'best work' and your comments about why it was chosen.
  - Use this best work as the standard against which their subsequent work is judged. From time to

time, compare, with your child, any new work against the criteria listed above. If it is not up to standard, the work might be redone (unless a special reason applies).

- When the writing has improved let the child tell you why. You might supply some special privilege as an incentive (even a calligraphy set for those becoming keen and proud). The better work could then become the new benchmark.

• For the younger writer, praise every effort at writing and focus on what is right rather than what they've done wrong. This encourages positive improvement.

• Provide a variety of ideas for them to write about — from writing about themselves to fantasy to pretend stories. Keep a list of stories.

• Talk at home about a topic that the child may be able to use the next day at school. Encourage a little practice at home so they will have more success at school.

Tips from teachers

✍ 'I've found that my class take much more pride with their writing if the page is decorated or illustrated, if it's poetry or if it's to be published, displayed and seen by others.'

✍ 'If getting kids to express thoughts and ideas in writing is the goal, rather than who is the neatest writer, then use the computer. Most kids love the computer.'

✍ 'In our preschool class we set up a writing corner with a posting box for the "letters" they wrote. Others may not understand them but I couldn't believe how much interest it generated and how much more they wanted to write and draw.'

Spelling problems

Any language that insists that o-n-c-e spells 'once' has to be hard going for young kids, migrants, or kids who can't see word patterns in their mind's eye. Spelling and reading are closely related, but not identical; reading only calls for the recognition of words (such as 'once'), but spelling poses the harder task of correct recall. If a child cannot recall a word to spell it, it's not just laziness — some can't work out the sounds, while others can't work out the teacher, but every one of them deserves help.

The best way to help develop good spelling is to provide plenty of good, fun books from the early picture book stage so the letters and patterns keep hammering away at the memory. By the age of 3 many children can recognise their own names. By 5, if children have taught themselves to write their first name, they will probably be problem-free.

If the patterns are just not sticking and tempers at homework time are becoming frayed, then it may be helpful to share that frustration with the teacher and ask for some better strategies. Raising your voice or blood pressure can be guaranteed to raise poorer spellers.

If you want to give your children some fun spelling games, ask at your local educational book supplier.

Spelling problem checklist

Look at a story your 'problem speller' has written and try to pick up the pattern of errors. Remember that all young kids have a spelling 'problem' as they try to cope with the vagaries of our language and its many complex rules, so don't be making them anxious when they don't need to be. However, primary kids could be considered to have a spelling problem if they have one or more of the following difficulties:

- Learn words but can't remember them days or weeks later
- Can only remember a list if the words are kept in the same order

- Spell words differently at different times
- Spell words as they sound but can't remember what they look like
- Can't see errors in spelling
- Can't break a word into parts or syllables
- Can recall sounds but can't recall symbols or combinations
- Use incorrect pronunciation in spelling (e.g. 'fin' for 'thin')
- Confuse the order of letters in spelling (e.g. 'gril' for 'girl')

Error	Possible solution
Good phonic attempts, e.g. 'dorter' for 'daughter'	Use word error flashcards and lots of reading to cement correct letter patterns
Poor phonic attempts, e.g. 'mothu' for 'mother'	Help to learn word families; teach the child to listen carefully; play 'sound detective' games (e.g. which word sounds different — thin, thin, fin, thin?)
Makes letter transpositions, e.g. 'gril' 'for girl'	Play word drill games; work on root blends (e.g. '—ir' in girl); use gimmicky memory aids (e.g. 'I are a girl')
Makes auditory errors, e.g. 'fin' for 'thin'	Tape-record the child reading and let the child pick out the errors; practise correct speech into a tape-recorder
Shows handwriting reversals, e.g. 'bug' for 'dug'	Use gimmicky memory aids to help the child remember the difference (e.g. 'bat before ball')

Error	Possible solution
Repetition, e.g. 'positition'	Provide self-correction incentives such as 5 minutes extra TV time for each spelling error they spot for themselves; practise re-reading words
Unclassifiable, e.g. 'dta' for 'daughter'	Give easier work and praise for success; practise listening to word sequences

DO

✓ Do encourage all attempts at spelling, e.g. 'have a go at ...'

✓ Do make spelling fun — play games.

✓ Do use the method 'look, say, cover, write, check' as a strategy to teach spelling words at home.

✓ Do insist on clear pronunciation of the word—this might make it easier to spell (e.g. 'ask' is often pronounced 'aks' or 'think' as 'fink').

✓ Do use an alphabet strip with pictures to assist young spellers to find the sound they need.

✓ Do focus on achievable words first — success breeds success.

✓ Do show the kids how to use dictionaries, encyclopaedias and thesauruses.

✓ Do play detective games with words, e.g. 'find words that rhyme with...', words that begin or end with the same sound, little words inside big words, words that sound the same but are spelt differently.

✓ Do play word games that focus on sounds of words (e.g. Junior Scrabble, Boggle, Wonderwords, I Spy, junior crosswords).

✓ Do fill your child's world with print (e.g. share story books, kitchen reminders, bedroom wall-hanging of verse, etc.) — the more the child sees the word, the more likely it is that the spelling will imprint over time on the mind.

✓ **Do** encourage e-mail and kids' Internet (monitored) chat lines — it is this type of functional use of spelling that is much more likely to have children motivated to find the right spelling so they can interact with each other without embarrassment.

DON'T

✗ **Don't** immediately tell your child the correct spelling — tempting and all as that may be, it will encourage spelling dependency habits that could last a lifetime and put similar demands on the teacher. Some parents and teachers use a 3-step process (columns on the page) — the child's first attempt, the second attempt after consulting a dictionary or other spelling source, and then the teacher's input (if needed).

✗ **Don't** cross out errors — for poor spellers this is very discouraging and makes them reluctant to write at all. Some teachers will put a line under the word, some suggest circling the word so the child knows there's a problem to be solved and can research (as above) for the correct answer.

Mathematics problems

Just the dull, flat sound of the word 'maths' can depress anyone who doesn't get a thrill from mental gymnastics with figures and numbers. I suppose modern kids can get by with less drill and more calculators, but when it comes to advanced maths the best machines in the world won't work unless you know what you are asking of them — and that takes understanding.

One of the biggest problems with today's maths is not the content but the vocabulary — the new words. That leads to much family friction over the 'old way' or the 'new way', when the difference is often in the words more than the way. Check with the teacher or even ask for a maths training night so you can help at home without confusing the kids.

All kids enjoy learning to count; they find the rhythm and precision very satisfying. Number drill, tables and rote learning are still very useful tools for children to possess. But there are many other ways parents can help kids too. Every time you ask kids to put something back where it belongs, or sort out cutlery, or silver and gold coins, or sock pairs, they're learning to put things in groups or classes — and that's maths. Even knowing in which drawer to find shirts, pants and socks is a form of maths. Organising their packing for holidays, packing the car boot, organising trips, managing time to play/work, getting ready for school on time, saving pocket money to buy things, predicting what will happen if/when ... that's maths, too, and it can be fun.

Most kids under 7 do need concrete aids like fingers or counters to learn maths, and even some older kids with a mild maths-delay problem will benefit from aids. They will switch to abstract calculation automatically when their brains can handle it, but premature pressure will make them both hate maths and perform very poorly.

Maths is one special area that can be easily and tangibly helped by computer assistance. Computers go at the right pace, they're very forgiving, they don't get frustrated and they work at individual levels for every child.

Some teachers swear by series such as 'Maths Made Easy' (available on CD-ROM), which offers children the chance to select from the menu of activities they need further work in (e.g. fractions) with different disks for each and every grade of primary school. But there are so many series around, you'd be wise to link up with what's being used in your children's school.

However, most children respond best to personal, professional one-to-one help with an individualised program designed by their teacher and/or tutor — preferably working together.

Maths problem checklist

By the age of 5:

- Can't rote count to 10
- Can't count simple objects like blocks up to 5
- Can't keep to the correct counting order
- Can't tell which names go with which numbers up to 10
- Mixes up colours
- Mixes up shapes
- Coins are all just pieces of money, with no difference in value

By the age of 7:

- Writes numbers back to front
- Hates doing maths homework
- Can't understand the difference between big and little, under and over, or first and last
- Friends and classmates seem further ahead
- Can only calculate with his or her fingers
- Still doesn't know the days of the week
- Has no real idea of time
- Has difficulty following a set of instructions

CASE STUDY
Andy

Andy was always good at drama and English, but hopeless at maths. When he was brought in for assessment and tutoring, his father mentioned that he had had a similar problem, which was why he'd gone in for law. We joked (with a touch of envy on my part) that surely lawyers needed to know how much they were banking. Dave just laughed and said that that was what his accountant was for! Fortunately, Dave got help for Andy before his problem had become a huge mathematical chip on his shoulder.

When we last reviewed progress Andy was in the middle ability maths class at high school.

Tips from teachers

✎ Play lots of games with the kids such as Ludo, Snakes and Ladders, Bingo, etc.

✎ Encourage help with shopping — prices, quantities, even locations of goods.

✎ Never say, 'I wasn't any good either' or 'I hated maths too'. This tells the child that it's okay to dislike or fail. A positive attitude works wonders.

✎ Comment from a maths coordinator: 'Maths is very much an applied subject these days with lots of equipment involved (e.g. scales, stopwatches). Some teachers use and enjoy maths texts but I find the books too repetitive on exercises and some of their activities not workable in the classroom so I tend to use a bit from a variety of books and my own experience. Teachers should let parents know at the start of the year how they can help with maths. Certainly if the kids are having a problem then parents should get early advice before the kids lose confidence.'

Concentration problems

One of the silliest comments on a school report card is the old 'could do better if he concentrated'! That's like saying 'could do better if he improved'! Concentration simply helps join the links in a chain of thought. It's a little like an internal telephone cabling system with electric circuits crisscrossing the brain; the thought won't linger if the charge is too weak, if the connections become confused, if a child's wiring is just too weak to carry the load or if it's hooked into another channel. That is, there are two sources of concentration loss.

Internal distracters — some kids can't screen out the irrelevant thoughts and become very distracted; they can't select or prioritise what's important and what's not. This is a little bit like the feeling most of us experience when we're falling asleep or daydreaming.

External distracters — stimulation from sights, sounds, movement, vibrations, smell and touch can make us lose our focus on what we were thinking about. Children with this problem become like 'stimulus slaves' — they can't screen out stimulation, they might be distracted by the clock ticking or a classmate moving. An academically weak child, already struggling with the work, doesn't need much in the way of kids calling out, brushing past, getting out of their seats, putting hands up, etc. to be distracted.

So often parents and teachers will label kids who are not concentrating as 'lazy', but in my experience laziness is often the result or symptom of a problem, not its cause. For example, I'm not a particularly clever mechanic — I can't see how and where things fit together nearly as well as mechanically minded people can. I'm sure that if I had to face a 12-year course in advanced mechanics, day in and day out, as kids with learning problems do, then my concentration would soon lapse and teachers would be calling me four-letter words like 'lazy'. What usually happens is that we switch off when something doesn't turn our brains on.

Concentration problems checklist

There are many reasons why children lose concentration, but if your child is having any of the problems on this list, then it's worth having it checked:

- Easily distracted by noises, movement, colour or novelty
- Frequently loses eye contact
- Unable to stick at any one activity for long
- Makes interruptions that have nothing to do with the topic of conversation
- Never seems to listen
- School reports repeatedly mention how easily distracted the child is

69

But be careful. Some children concentrate poorly on what others want them to, not because they can't focus or even don't want to, but because they are overfocused on something they're watching (e.g. football) or doing (e.g. computer games) or making (e.g. modelling) or thinking (e.g. why friend didn't play with them that day).

How to help
- Have the child medically/physically checked for any physical problem such as fatigue, poor hearing, ear infections, a thyroid problem or hearing loss.
- If the child seems to be forever losing messages, forgetting what they were saying or showing a tendency to go off into a trance, also ask for a neurological check-up as there might just be some odd disrhythmic or disruptive brainwave patterns (spiking).
- If that gets the all-clear, then ask for a psychological check, either through the school counsellor or guidance officer, or with a private educational psychologist. The reasons for this are to see whether:
  - the child is having trouble keeping up intellectually (intelligence assessment);
  - their mind is too easily distracted (attention deficit assessment);
  - there is any emotional overload or interference coming from problems at home or in the playground (stressor assessment);
  - there are communication patterns at home such as nagging parent, shouting, noisy household, parent taking over responsibility (home style assessment).
  - If concentration is poor because the child's work is too hard, then ask the teacher for suitable work — no one goes to school to fail.
  - If poor concentration is just a bad habit, then teach the child some 'habit busters' such as letting them work out the best spot to concentrate. At school it may be near the front where they can't see other

kids; at home it may be in the child's own bedroom unless they can prove otherwise.

- If high school kids are keen to improve concentration, here are some ways they can help themselves:
  - Diet check — to make sure their intake includes plenty of 'brain food' and not food that overstimulates or agitates them, such as chocolates, cola drinks, food colourings, preservatives, etc.
  - Study style check — when doing homework they can start by setting a watch alarm for 15 minutes. If they make it to the bell they can work beyond and record how much overtime was done. Then they can take a 5-minute break and go back to work for another 14 minutes, then 13, then 12, and so on. Each time they should record any overtime. When they've finished the work the overtime is added up and can be traded in on the same number of extra minutes to watch TV, time on the phone, time out at the weekend or whatever is agreed.
  - Some students pick the most boring subject, usually the one from which they are most easily distracted, record the number of times they were distracted and try to reduce the score.

CASE STUDY

Tim

Tim had been in lots of minor trouble at school for calling out, not working, not concentrating and being disruptive. His school reports were a disaster. He was blamed for being naughty when, in fact, he had a concentration problem which was out of his control. In some cases medication is needed to deal with such a problem, but we managed to avoid it this time with the help of a keen teacher and understanding parents.

Despite the comments on all his report cards, Tim was not aware that he was not working, so we set up a simple program with his teacher's help. His teacher started a 'red/green' system; a card with a red circle on one side and a green circle on the other was kept on the left-hand top corner of Tim's desk. When he lost concentration his teacher flipped the card to red and moved it across one space to the right, but no big fuss was made; when he worked hard the card was flipped back to green and moved left a space. Tim's job was to keep that card to the left of the centre of his desk—if he did, rewards followed, if not, he had to miss out on some free time to catch up on work.

Part of the encouragement was that if he did well, Tim would be allowed to keep something on his desk like the other kids did, but which had proved too much of a temptation before (e.g. rulers, biros and pencil sharpeners). His teacher and parents made a point of giving him instructions only once, but made sure they got his attention first. And it seems to be working.

Tips from teachers

✍ Teachers had no consensus of advice on this issue — their suggestions were many and varied and included eye/ear checks, short activities, discussion with teacher, time limits with rewards, removal of distractions, paediatric check, diet check, good sleep routines, clear rules when working and assessment by school counsellor.

Worriers and perfectionists

'Worry-warts' are kids who suffer from free-floating anxiety. These kids know that for every step taken a new door opens, but what worries them is what's behind the door, and what happened to the door that just shut behind them! Many kids are born worriers, but many also live in a house that oozes worry and anxiety to the point that the kids just soak it up.

Many of the symptoms are picked up under 'Stressed kids' (below) but from the time these kids get up to the time they fall asleep (and that's often hard too), their little lives are one big worry after another.

Perfectionists are made in heaven, often moulded in a fussy home and rounded off at school, but they are hard to live with, particularly for the person hiding inside the perfectionist. They must have everything right, refuse to hand work in if there is a single error, avoid anything that they can't accomplish perfectly, are critical of mistakes in self or others, never know when enough is enough, spend hours on homework and assignments.

How to help the worriers
- Make sure home is a place where your children can laugh or play off their anxiety and that they know how to relax and unwind.
- Encourage conversation, and make sure you listen. Acknowledge even the smallest achievements; make sure your children see problems as challenges that can be solved together; insert some humour whenever possible; put up with childish, happy jokes; take an interest in their interests; and, most importantly, make sure their time is unhurried and has some built-in 'down-time' each day.
- Encourage activities that are soothing, such as listening to music, being stroked or cuddled, massaged with oils, playing with warm soapy water in the kitchen sink, playing with pets, colouring in or reading.
- Encourage joining in after school activities (e.g. dancing, music, sport — whatever and wherever their interests lie) to release their worries and distract their minds.

If you use therapy make sure that it focuses not on why the child is worried, because kids who carry an anxiety disorder hardly ever know why, but on what can be done about it. Many 'worry tossing' tactics are outlined in detail in my book *Who'd Be a Parent?: The Manual That Should Have Come With the Kids.* Among my favourites are the following.

1. The 'What If' Worry Winning Game:
    - Kids work out some ways to handle some of their fears so they become winners, e.g. 'what if a bully was to say he'd get you after school?', etc.
    - When they've come up with possibilities, you add a few of yours, they choose the best to suit their circumstances and that builds up their feeling that it was worth sharing their worry and that a worry shared is a worry spared.
    - In other words, they become what Stephen Covey (author of *Seven Habits of Highly Effective Families*) calls 'inside out' kids rather than 'outside in' kids. That is, *they* make the move and they force the outcome, rather than hopelessly and anxiously waiting for the 'fickle finger of fate to crook her damning digit'.

2. Play the 'as if' game. For the kids who feel trapped by worry I'll sometimes ask them to act as if they were one of their friends who is very confident, and notice the difference. Or if they're animal lovers, I might ask them to feel like their favourite animal.

3. Have fun with a desensitising game called the 'Worry Winning Ladder'.
    - Kids list or tell you all their worries.
    - These are each rated out of 10 by the worrier, with highest scores to the biggest fears.
    - The fears are then arranged on a ladder with the lowest-scored worries on the bottom rung. (Make sure that the lowest is such a little worry — 1 out of 10 — that they can't help but succeed.)
    - The kids work their way up the ladder, but they need some worry-beating aid to make it easier (worry dolls, squeeze ball, images, power stone, etc.).
    - If any step is too hard, break it down into smaller steps

so again success is ensured.

4.   'Give It a Rest': Try a worry-unloading game. Have a special drawer in some little keepsake or jewellery box which you mark as the 'Give It a Rest' drawer. Before bedtime let your children draw or write what's worrying them and put it in the drawer for thinking about the next day, not then. I use those little worry dolls or guardian angels in the same way— give each doll a name and a special job (like making sure Mum doesn't die, or whatever else the child is worried about), standing the dolls on Blu-Tack on their dressing table, so that each doll carries a special worry.

5.   Have a calming corner somewhere out of the way. It must be a corner — no noise or interruptions — where anyone can go when stressed to listen to soft music, read a book or magazine, do a puzzle, brush hair, or anything that helps them unwind on their own.

6.   'Worry Burner': For a bit of reverse psychology on uptight kids needing a tension reliever use an energy outlet such as the rhythm of the trampoline or just let them burn it off somewhere safe like a park or beach.

7.   Be playful in the way you handle kids' worries so the atmosphere as well as the message helps them to handle their own anxieties. That means parents need to find fun in their own lives, taking time to play and re-energise their systems. That not only reduces their anxiety but it helps kids find ways to handle their problems more playfully and less stressfully. The best results will come if we get the anxiety out of the air. The problem is that worry works — as one little kid said to me, 'When I worry real hard the thing I worry about never happens'.

How to help perfectionists

•   Have a conference with the teacher and agree to reward effort, imperfect and incomplete work only. Don't worry about standards slipping, these kids provide their own pressure. For instance, see if they can be strong enough to get work wrong and not let it bother them, or strong enough to stop doing something they haven't quite finished and not worry about it.

- Encourage messy play, getting dirty, water play, rhythm, playing with pets — anything to get their bodily defences down — as I find many of these kids are fearful of messy or free-for-all play.

- Be aware of how you use praise. Parental pride in a toddler's talent can lead to extravagant praise and raise the mistaken belief in the child that they should be able to do anything. Make sure you always:
  - praise action not ego
  - praise effort not just success
  - praise ability to handle failure as much as success
  - praise sharing, waiting, the ability to handle being second best, and other social skills vital for a happy childhood.

- Let the child write out a 'permission note' giving them permission not to be perfect at some particular stressful school activity that day.

- Examine your own behaviour. Do you highlight performance success or enjoyment? Are you overcritical of your own performance? Do you do too much for the children, implying that they can't do it for themselves? Are you intolerant of their failures? Are you trying to raise the perfect kid?

- Applaud and enjoy the efforts your children make even in things they don't do well.

- Perfectionism is an attitude, not an achievement, so use imaginary characters or true stories about kids who have had to confront similar problems and how they dealt with them.

- Continually model, even if it hurts, the easy acceptance of self-inflicted mistakes and the mistakes of others. In other words, learn to go easy on yourself if you want the kids to do likewise. I couldn't count the number of perfectionists I've treated who have a parent who is totally obsessed with cleanliness, tidiness and fastidiousness around the house.

CASE STUDY
Ben

Worry casts a big shadow on little kids. In fact, Ben's mum was worried about all the things Ben was worried about — wetting his bed (although he'd only wet it once), getting yelled at, getting his spelling wrong, getting his work finished, sore tummies ... in fact, life itself.

I had to explain to his mother that kids become worried when their parents worry and this leads to a convoluted situation where everyone's worrying about worrying all the time.

So, before his mum could tell me any more worries, Ben and I started working out some tactics. We rated all his worries on a scale of 1 to 10; we found that imagining leaves falling gently one after another to the bottom of his tummy helped him to relax; we lined up a tutor to help his bad reading and spelling problem; and his mum decided to try to concentrate on what good things were happening rather than on the bad things that might.

But sometimes I wonder how much I achieved. As Ben and his mum were leaving, I happened to mention, as a throw-away line, that worry can sometimes cast a big shadow. Mum stopped in her tracks: 'Oh, that's another thing, doctor, Ben's always worried about shadows and the dark. Should I worry about that?' Kids may never listen to parents, but they rarely fail to copy.

Stressed kids

'Stress' became the buzzword of the 90s, describing the sense of overload that adults were feeling as they tried to cope in a world on overload. Yet for some reason we treated stress as a purely adult problem, unaware that children are even more vulnerable, with less maturity to handle it all. But an interesting thing about stress is that it's a response to how we see things which depends not on fact but on feeling — how we perceive a problem. For instance, going to a kid's birthday party may be fun for a child who expects to eat and play a lot, but not so much fun for another child scared stiff no one will talk to them. Research shows that parents often miscalculate and misunderstand what is stressful to kids. For example, parents rate the birth of a new sibling as much more stressful to the other children than children rate it, whereas children rate parental conflict much higher than adults do. The fact is that school is considered by children as one of the most stressful domains of their experience — not necessarily because of any major incident but more often because of the net effect of lots of minor stressors. Where young children find it difficult is that they're not mentally mature enough to analyse what it is that is causing the stress, let alone understand the changes which need to be made to reduce it.

Top stressors for children
- Parental divorce/separation
- Repeating a year at school (much more so for upper

primary or high school students)
- Wetting pants in class
- Being suspected of lying
- Poor report card
- Ridiculed in class
- Academic failure
- Social failure — not selected in a sporting team, not invited to parties, not invited to sit next to someone in class, etc.
- Family failure — not matching up to brighter, faster or smarter school mates or siblings
- Chronic illness, depression or conflict in the family
- Conflict with a teacher, or getting in trouble for poor work or poor behaviour
- Financial failure — not having enough money to go on school excursions, concerts, to have the same shoes as their friends, to buy food from the canteen, etc.

According to research in the 1991 *Psychological Reports Journal*, children (aged 8 to 12) from non-traditional families (step-parents, single parents, foster parents) report a much greater degree of school-related stress than children from traditional families, regardless of sex, ethnic background and type of school program.

Identifying signs of stress
Research shows that parents have difficulties identifying a child under stress until the stress is quite serious — perhaps indicated by extreme violence, suicidal ideation or self-harm. Below is a checklist for identifying stress. There may be cause for concern if your child presents with more than 7 of these factors, or if one or two are quite extreme:
- Sleeping late (even on weekends) or insomnia
- Avoiding school
- Fighting with both siblings and friends
- Displaying hostility to teachers and other adults
- General irritability and sensitivity to people and the environment

- Complaints of physical illness (stomach-aches, headaches)
- Onset of bedwetting or soiling
- Nightmares
- Increase in clumsiness and accidents
- Trembling, nervous tics (twitches)
- Teeth grinding
- Prolonged loss of appetite
- Stuttering
- Repeated movements, such as rocking or headbanging

If you have the feeling that many of these symptoms are often associated with 'naughty kids' rather than with 'stressed kids', in a sense you'd be right — because many of the kids suffering stress are misdiagnosed as 'naughty'. Far too often, parents, teachers and health professionals treat the symptoms of the stressed child by targeting the disruptive behaviour rather than treating the cause.

How to help the 'stressed child' or help prevent stress

- From an early age introduce novelty and new experiences as this helps kids learn how to cope with change — go to new cinemas, playgrounds, visit different friends, and involve them in some group such as Cubs or Brownies where excursions and new experiences are regular occurrences. Encourage the kids to make changes in their bedrooms and to do different jobs around the house.
- In their schoolwork, look for effort rather than perfection. Children soon learn it is difficult to be 'the best' at anything — there is always another child who is faster, stronger, smarter or better. Praising the child who tries their best is the surest way to ensure their self-esteem can be maintained regardless of how they perform in any activity.
- Help them find the sports, activities and hobbies that they enjoy. That way they won't write themselves off as

inadequate if they struggle in some areas of schoolwork. What's more, if one area runs into trouble (e.g. from a sporting injury), they have other areas to fill the gap.

- Provide good models of behaviour — if you aren't coping with stress, how do you expect the kids to manage? Show your children that any stress can be dealt with in a constructive way — how to be problem-solvers, not just problem-livers. Not only will you help yourself, but you'll also help your child.

- Create special down-time, cuddle-time, play-time, doing-nothing-much-time, so the whole family can relax. Switch off the television and the radio, play some quiet relaxing music, burn oils, play a board game, draw, cook together, massage ... whatever makes the family feel good.

- Try to work out what the stressors in the child's life might be. For younger kids this may mean keeping notes on when and where it's at its worst. For older kids, you can set up a grouch list of everything that makes them feel 'yukky' and they can give each one a rating out of 10. Remember, if you can identify what has made your child stressed, then you're halfway to solving the problem.

  Stress is simply a part of life for every individual— wherever they are, whatever they do and whatever age they are. Our job as parents is to help kids find ways to handle it so they can face life confidently, comfortable in their own coping system.

Tips from teachers

✍ A surprising number of teachers commented that problems in organisation and time management were the big stressors for the children in their class — help kids with those aspects and we may have better coping kids.

Underactive or 'lazy' learners

No kids are more frustrating to teach or help with homework than 'lazy' learners. Sometimes it seems that their pens are too heavy to lift, their heads too heavy to hold up, their thoughts too heavy to worry about schoolwork, or that life is just too heavy altogether.

Although these kids may be easier to manage than overactive children, their learning problems are often more serious and more far-reaching. The mistake we often make is to think that their laziness is the cause of their problem, whereas, in fact, it is often the symptom or even the result of another problem.

'Laziness' checklist

Many kids are diagnosed as 'lazy' or underactive when the problem could well be a physical one. Your school-aged kid is probably not just 'lazy' if he/she:

- is underactive at all times, not just at school
- is listless and unable to concentrate
- lacks interest in playing sport
- never joins in games at recess or lunchtime
- prefers activities that require no energy
- whinges or grizzles consistently
- needs more than 12 hours' sleep a night
- is reluctant to get up, even at weekends

These are just a few of the symptoms which are often labelled as laziness, but which could well have medical significance and need urgent attention from your local doctor.

How to help
- Find out just where the child is being lazy — if it is at school, try to find out why; if it is at home, try to discover the causes there; but if it is all the time, consult a doctor. A full medical check can catch

problems such as allergies, glandular fever, low-grade infections, chronic fatigue syndrome, thyroid problems, kidneys, diabetes, anaemia, or other ailments that could be causing the lack of energy.

- If the child is always daydreaming then a neurological test may be valuable to discover if there is any disrhythmic activity; if you receive the all-clear there, then consult a psychologist who may discover an emotional problem that has caused the drop in effort.
- Don't forget that hatred of school or sport or problems in getting along with other kids can cause a child to 'drop out'.
- Very achievement-orientated homes can also be a factor. 'Laziness' is a highly successful countermove against parents who expect too much. Children who can't outpower powerful parents will often use passive resistance. That way no one can ever accuse them of answering back, being rude or showing temper. The hidden aim is to frustrate rather than cooperate.
- Re-energise the child who has lost heart by opening your heart. Cut through the excuses and be as supportive as possible until the child has rediscovered their own strength and energy.

CASE STUDY
Dave

Twelve-year-old Dave walked gawkily into my clinic, slumped down into a chair and, with his head down, made sure he avoided eye contact. The note from his father said, 'The kid is bone idle'. We started to investigate.

Actually Dave was very talented: he had a brilliant vocabulary, incredible comprehension, was terrific at maths and, in fact, fell into the top 1 per cent of the students. The problem was that Dave wasn't very good at practical skills, which meant that Dave and his father just weren't on the same wavelength. His father was a top electrician, big on 'right-brain' talent and very practical.

His father was bitterly disappointed in the boy, and Dave knew it. He had failed the 'family fitness test'. He wasn't lazy, just lonely.

Once Dave's father recognised the reasons for the rift, his opposition diminished overnight and he started to accept the boy as he was, not as he had wanted him to be. Dave and his father are still very different characters but now they can be good friends.

Tips from teachers

✍ The majority of teachers suggested a health check and psychological check, others suggested rewards for effort and discussion with the teacher.

✍ 'My own son was lazy. I think it was because I was so busy I'd end up doing things for him to get them done. When I realised I was making him lazy I decided to put as much effort in as he did. If he hadn't done much to help out on his chores, I'd just not have time to help him with his homework or make anything special for dinner. I remember one time he was particularly offended when I had had to put up with his half-baked efforts so I half-baked his dinner and said, "Oh, it'll do, son".'

Overactive learners

Just as some kids tend to be less active than others, for whatever reason, so some kids tend to be more active than others. But at what point is this behaviour overactive, and is there any difference between overactive and hyperactive? Well, obviously much is in the eye of the beholder, but there are some differences.

Overactive	Hyperactive
Can still concentrate when requested or interested	Is rarely able to concentrate except when watching television or when extremely active
Has reasonably stable moods	Is very moody; has rapid mood swings
Can still relax and unwind when necessary	Rarely relaxes — is on the go constantly
Has few associated problems	Has many associated problems (e.g. learning difficulties, aggression)

Overactive learners don't really pose a problem because their concentration is there and they can modify their behaviour on request; in fact, their energy and vitality can be a real asset in and out of the classroom. Hyperactive learners do pose some problems for the teacher and family as their behaviour is often associated with a condition well known as ADHD — Attention Deficit with Hyperactivity Disorder. Although it is not unusual to find children with ADHD who do not present as hyperactive (maybe just inattentive or impulsive), nevertheless hyperactivity is a very common attribute of a disorder which in itself is still open to a lot of debate. I have no doubt about the existence and impact on the family of such a condition, nor does Professor Barkley, Director of Psychology and Professor of Psychiatry and Neurology at the University of Massachusetts and a world authority on the subject. In his article in the September 1998 issue of *Scientific American* he pinpoints areas of the brain which are clearly implicated in ADHD-type behaviour (poor self-control, inattention, hyperactivity, impulsivity, etc.). Brain imaging techniques have found that the prefrontal lobe (responsible for 'editing' behaviour, resisting distractions and developing an awareness of self and time) in children with

ADHD was significantly smaller than for other children. Researchers have also found that the cell mass deep in the brain-stem responsible for helping kids switch off automatic responses and for coordinating brain messages was also much smaller in ADHD kids. But Professor Barkley also found that identical twins (with identical genes) were 11–18 times more likely to have ADHD if their twin did. An English research team also found, from their huge study of ADHD children, that 'up to 80 per cent of the differences in attention, hyperactivity and impulsivity between people with ADHD and those without the disorder can be explained by genetic factors'. By contrast, premature birth, maternal alcohol and tobacco use, exposure to lead, brain injuries, poor diet and bad parenting collectively contribute to only 20–30 per cent of the problem. The affected genes appear to make it hard for dopamine, a chemical responsible for carrying messages throughout the brain, to act effectively, particularly in the prefrontal section which controls or edits all behaviour. The result is that kids with ADHD have real difficulty in self-control ... and so their behaviour is very frustrating, annoying and irritating to others.

Often the behaviour is more of a problem at school, where kids are faced with so much competing information, so many distractions and so much abstract information. School report cards are likely to repeatedly mention 'poor concentration', 'poor listening' 'disruptive behaviour', 'interrupts other pupils', 'never finishes anything', etc. At home, when these children are active, in front of a computer or video or TV, or doing something with their hands, there may not be a problem.

Professor Barkley has also identified several common dimensions allied to ADHD, including the following:

Behavioural	Social
Fiddles, can't sit still, is easily distracted, restless, noisy, loud, impulsive.	Has few friends, is disobedient, tells lies, shoots from the lip, a high risk taker, argues.

Academic	Social
Underachieves, has reading and spelling problems.	Has few friends, is disobedient, tells lies, shoots from the lip, a high risk taker, argues.

Emotional	Cognitive
Has low self-esteem, is easily upset, suffers depression, is excitable and easily frustrated, displays variable moods.	Impulsive thinker, poor listener, inattentive, shows some lack of conscience, unaware of consequences.

Of course, not every one of these characteristics is present in any one child, but there may be enough for you to say, 'Yes, that's my kid!' If it is, then you will notice that the problem and related symptoms affect more than just their level of general activity.

The condition can't be cured, although many do grow out of most symptoms, but there are two major ways to help these kids who lack self-control. If the problem is serious, one way is to provide medication that can boost their dopamine levels so the kids can function more 'normally'; research suggests that the majority of genuine ADHD kids do improve with medications such as Ritalin or Dexamphetamine. However, whether medicated or not, there are several key management principles:

- Take care of the simple things: slow down the pace of life at home; introduce steady and consistent routines; cut out any junk food; work out activities that might be soothing, e.g. having a bath, doing a puzzle or listening to music.
- Remember, these kids have big engines but poor brakes, so try steering your child in directions you prefer rather than blocking behaviour you don't like (e.g. 'Sammy, give me the pencil now, please!' will get better results than 'Sammy, stop stabbing your sister!').
- Remember that very few of these kids learn best in the abstract (the message gets lost too easily), so save your

voice and be practical. Teach by practice, praise, copying and correcting.

- Check whether food sensitivities are playing a part — cola drinks, tomato sauce, preservatives, colourings and flavourings are commonly blamed, but there are many others that could be implicated. For more information on dietary factors consult the section 'ADD — Attention Digested Disorder' in my book *Who'd Be a Parent?: The Manual That Should Have Come With the Kids*, or Sue Dengate's book, *Fed Up*.
- Be very clear, very firm and very consistent in directions to these kids so the brain's defective control mechanisms get maximum outside help.
- Work closely with the teachers to determine common rules, common attention refocusing methods, common routines, common expectations, and share what's working or not working in the child's management.
- For those wanting more information consult Ian Wallace's excellent book, *You and Your A.D.D. Child*, or Dr Geoff Kewley's new LAC publication, *Attention Deficit Hyperactivity Disorder*.

Sometimes the parents' methods of managing these kids are partly to blame, but given that parents of children with ADHD are 5 to 7 times more likely to also suffer from the same difficulty, then do we blame the grandparents or great-grandparents? If our answer is eugenics or selective breeding to rid us of defective genes, then just be careful — we might all get culled!

CASE STUDY
AJ

AJ had all the classic ADHD symptoms — fidgety, a poor listener, couldn't sit still, easily distracted, disruptive, never finished anything, and as you'd expect was driving his parents insane. So we tried some behavioural tactics such as strict rules, practising behaviour they wanted, and using water and music and trampoline to soothe his system. Then we checked food intolerances and found that AJ had several, but red colouring was his worst. Still his parents felt like the greatest failures in parentdom. Then we organised a trial on Ritalin and that worked wonders.

AJ became a different boy, improved in behaviour and schoolwork and went up in the class and in self-esteem — but football was the only exercise he yearned for. So Dad sponsored the footy team and that way got him in as a fumbly forward. But they noticed when they took him off his medication at weekends, as many do, that he was back to his old active self and actually ran, chased, tackled and played much better. It sure says something for the impact of food colourings for some kids, doesn't it? Anyhow, Dad thought that if AJ could make a go of footy, he might give cricket a go for summer — reckons he'll try chamomile tea at half-time!

Tips from teachers

✍ I've seen many correctly diagnosed children with ADHD improve on medication (and I've seen many incorrectly diagnosed and medicated too). Recently one parent, who knew I had some sympathy for her situation, sent me these lovely words: 'ADHD children are a bit like a caterpillar. Not many can appreciate their inherent beauty and, let's face it, they often leave behind a trail of turmoil and destruction. But if you nurture them, and make sure they don't get squashed along the way, wings with the most brilliant kaleidoscope of colours will slowly unfold. And they are ready to fly.'

'Slow' learners

For kids who can't keep up, school looms as a sentence of 10 years' hard labour with a bit of time off if they are expelled for bad behaviour. It's not surprising that slow learners can become very resentful and very anti-school. In a sense it is like battling every day for 10 years, only to be told you are a failure

— but to keep on trying anyway. Not many kids can do that unless they have adults in their lives who are very supportive, a school that values effort and character as much as intellect, and a skill or talent that can compensate and make them feel that life is worth the effort.

Slow learners frequently are a little behind other kids their own age in learning to count, draw, recite, listen, write, talk or read. And sometimes they may even be behind in physical skills such as dressing, catching and doing up shoes, but please remember that physical skills are not reliable indicators. I should add that some delay for any one of these skills is not an indication of slow learning but of individual style: boys, for instance, are notoriously slower talkers than girls.

The next indication can usually be found in school reports. Comments such as 'having difficulty', 'poor concentration', or even 'tries hard', could well mean that schoolwork is a real struggle and action needs to be taken quickly.

How to help
- If your child is of preschool age follow the suggestions for 'Special needs children', in Chapter 1 and Appendix 1.
- If your child is of school age and you're concerned, or they are performing way below siblings at the same age, then check with the teacher to see if progress there is below average — and don't be put off by the 'They'll catch up' line.
- If the teacher is concerned, ask for an intellectual assessment by the school counsellor or local psychologist — this is not just an IQ test, it's the equivalent of a medical overhaul to see how your child's brain is ticking and how best to tailor a program to suit their profile.
- On the basis of that assessment ask the school for a two-way plan of action that will not only help the child's weaknesses but also find the strengths so they need never feel a total failure.

- On the home front that plan of action must *not* be an extra dose of schoolwork, although a tutor can often work wonders with skills and morale. Instead it must include opportunities to achieve in non-school areas in which they show a flair. There are many talents other than schoolwork (music, sport, maths, spatial, practical, animal care, computers, gardening, common sense, collecting, furniture making, modelling, money making, old people care, drawing or painting, etc.). Each child is unique and each child brings to their family some talents that can be the core of their self-worth and the springboard for profitable employment.
- Remember that kids can be cruel to anyone who is different or weaker, so be prepared for some teasing and name calling (e.g. 'spas', 'idiot' 'drop-kick'). Help with some teasing tossing tactics (see page 121), and mention it to the teacher. Singling kids out for sympathy in class is not the way to help, as it highlights their weakness and invariably backfires. Instead, most modern teachers will work with the whole class on self-esteem raising activities designed to increase respect for each other and understanding of differences, and to find unique talents that can be profiled in the classroom. For social skills development suggestions see Chapter 4.
- Teaching slow learners often requires paying more attention to the practical side of learning, such as teaching with everyday examples and materials, handling abstract work in short sessions, and adjusting learning goals so that they are within reach. If the school, parent or tutor can adjust learning to suit a slow learner's needs and abilities there is no reason why a 'slow' learner can't win as many accolades as a 'fast' learner.

CASE STUDY
Karen

Have you ever thought what it's like to be a slow learner in a fast family? Karen was the eldest of three girls. She loved her family and her sisters but couldn't stand the fact that as they grew older her sisters were able to do her work better than she could.

When she asked her mum how to do something or how to spell a word her sisters always chimed in, not to be smart but just because they were enjoying their growing knowledge and wanted everyone to know how clever they were. Karen's parents changed the homework routine so that Karen had some privacy and could no longer be shown up by her sisters. They also made a rule that no one was to participate in anyone else's work unless invited.

But as she matured Karen knew she was falling further and further behind and by sixth class she hated school, wouldn't do any homework and had become very stressed. The breakthrough came at high school. Karen was the first sister there — she found new friends, took different subjects and was in a class with kids of her own ability. Her parents also discovered she was becoming a talented young chef. Her sisters enjoyed her new culinary skills and this won their respect. There was no more competition because the kids were now running different races.

Tips from teachers

✍ The majority of the teachers suggested building on the positive things that a child can do and concentrating on their strengths.
✍ 'I think I was a bit impatient with my slow learners. I suppose because I had to get through the curriculum and they were slowing me down and frustrating me. Then my own child turned out to be a slow learner and I realised how special she was, and while school just saw her as a problem, I saw her as the best thing in our lives. Since then I think I have a whole different attitude to kids who are struggling — I really try to help them enjoy school and feel part of the class. I'd hate them to feel they're failures as my daughter has so often done.'

'Fast' or gifted learners

No one wants their child to be a slow learner. Everyone wants 'fast' or what we term 'gifted' learners. But gifted learners are not any happier than an average child, they don't get better jobs, and they don't necessarily earn more money. Maybe we think that giftedness is next to godliness, or at least is divine proof that the parents had genetic genius.

In the school business there's a distinction made between a 'gift' and a 'talent'. Generally, giftedness is about nature's gifts of outstanding ability intellectually, physically, socially, sensorily or creatively. Gifts can go undeveloped if they are not nurtured properly; in the sections above I commented on how some gifted kids become lazy or underachieving if their abilities aren't nurtured properly. Likewise many parents and teachers label bright kids as gifted. As can be seen from the checklist below there are several features that distinguish gifted kids from bright kids.

The bright child	The gifted learner
Knows the answers	Asks the questions
Is interested in things	Is a highly curious explorer
Is focused and attentive	Is highly mentally and physically involved
Likes words	Uses a complex, often unusual, vocabulary
Has good ideas	Has flamboyant, silly ideas
Works hard	Mucks around, yet tests well
Answers the questions	Discusses in detail, elaborates
In the top group	A group of one beyond the others
Listens with interest	Shows strong feelings and opinions
Learns with ease	Knows already
6–8 repetitions for mastery	Mastery after 1–2 repetitions
Understands ideas	Develops abstract ideas
Enjoys peers	Prefers adult company
Grasps the meaning	Explores implications
Completes assignments	Starts projects
Copies accurately	Creates new designs
Enjoys school	Enjoys learning
A technician	An inventor
Adept at memorising	A great guesser
Enjoys simple clear logic	Thrives on complexity
Is pleased with own learning	Is highly self-critical

Although many parents like having gifted kids, it's the bright kids who usually fit in better and make the top students. Gifted kids often have a very hard row to hoe in life and need special understanding. There is also a tendency for parents (and some teachers) to equate superior academic performance with giftedness. All children are gifts and all children are talented in some little way. It's also about time we recognised and respected other gifted learners in areas such as mathematics, music, art, performing arts, sport and social intelligence.

Unfortunately many gifted and talented children become what is termed 'underachievers', never reaching anywhere near their potential.

In an analysis of gifted 'underachievers', Sylvia Rimm and Barbara Lowe found that, in comparison to gifted 'achievers', there were some differences in the home environment:

1. Underachieving children received exceptionally *high* levels of early attention, which can be interpreted as possibly making the child feel so special that they resented any intrusions into that image (e.g. the arrival of a new baby, starting school, the arrival of a step-parent). This hurt was often displayed in defiant or unproductive behaviour.
2. There was some inconsistency between parental roles. In 21 of the 22 families studied, one parent always took the disciplinarian role, while the other always took the protective, softer role, perhaps to balance things out.
3. The child showed dependence on parents to finish homework.
4. There was evidence of parental dissatisfaction, disorganisation and frustration with their careers and situation in life. Children from high-achieving families were not only more optimistic but more organised with their time, leaving spare time to devote to family interests and developing their independence.

How to help

It's most important to remember that gifted children are still children! Like all children they need soft and firm love, nurturing and training. Here are some do's and don'ts:

DO

✓   Do allow 'playing around' time. Children don't have to be 'gainfully' employed every waking moment. There should be time for daydreaming, clowning around, watching TV, reading comics, playing on the computer and lying on an unmade bed to contemplate the ceiling. Gifted children are usually creative children. And creativity doesn't happen on schedule. Creativity comes

95

from profitably 'playing around'.

✓ **Do** encourage gifted learners to follow up their hobbies, planning and striving for real mastery, rather than going through a lot of hobbies or collections in a short time.

✓ **Do** take your child to libraries and art galleries etc. If they feel free to explore the world through books, nature, science, prehistoric monsters, or anything else that takes their interest, it enhances their hunger for knowledge and skill.

✓ **Do** have good books, magazines, encyclopaedias, charts, maps, collections, etc. at home. It helps develop useful background knowledge.

✓ **Do** read biographies and introduce your child to people who have succeeded by persisting in the face of adversity. Show respect for hard work as well as innate ability.

✓ **Do** let gifted kids specialise early if they wish. There are fringe benefits in living with dinosaurs — kids will learn research skills, how to keep notes and records, discovering library catalogue systems and retrieval skills along the way.

✓ **Do,** within reason, let gifted kids try to do what they say they can. If their judgment is faulty, there is learning to be had from that too.

✓ **Do** praise your child for effort and trying, for the wonderful things done, even though the experiment may not have worked out as hoped. Enquiring minds must take intellectual risks and this needs encouragement and support.

✓ **Do** respect and enjoy the knowledge that gifted kids can bring to a discussion. Assume the kids intend to do the right thing, especially when questions of authority arise. Don't become defensive just because their logic challenges power-based management. Listening to their point of view doesn't mean you have to agree.

✓ **Do** help them to respect conventions. Gifted kids are

sometimes impatient of conventions of politeness, manner and courtesy, but they can be helped to rationally see the social advantages of such conventions and how they relate to respect for others.

✓ **Do** make links with associations. It's harder for schools to cater totally for gifted kids, so forge links with groups or teams that can cater to their special interests. One very important link to make is with the Gifted and Talented Children's Association. It runs camps, weekend workshops and information nights, and has lots of ideas to help the parents of gifted kids.

✓ **Do** consider mentoring. Mentoring links up the child with an expert, knowledgeable other person — adult or older child — who can inspire, guide, role-model and enhance the child's own current expertise. It may be arranged through the G&T Children's Association or the child's school, but any program should not be too structured and should be allowed to develop naturally. A mentor needs to be chosen carefully.

DON'T

✗ **Don't** compare your gifted child with other children. All children are unique and special in their own way and need to focus on their own abilities and not how they do with respect to others.

✗ **Don't** expect your gifted child to fulfil all of your own unachieved aspirations.

✗ Don't dismiss the Internet! (See 'Computers' on pages 233–238.)

Above all, enjoy your gifted child. Of all the problems children might have, giftedness is surely the best one! Gifted children are curious, enthusiastic, excited about new things and able to communicate at a sophisticated level early! Some of this is likely to rub off on all those lucky enough to know and love a gifted child.

Tips from teachers

✍ Almost every teacher surveyed expressed the same opinion — if you feel your child is gifted talk to the teacher or school counsellor for an objective opinion and, if appropriate, extension work (i.e. different work, not more of the same) can easily be provided.

Chapter 4

In the Playground

As far as kids are concerned the playground is where it all happens. Academic excellence, artistic accolades, musical majesty — all pale into insignificance compared to playground prowess. For some the playground is a platform to exhibit their sporting and social skills, for others it's purgatory. It's the playground rather than the classroom that is the nerve centre of the school and, from my discussions with kids, the amount of school time spent inside versus outside the classroom is in inverse proportion to the amount of time spent thinking about them. Tempting as it is to shield children from playground problems, we must remember that we are all basically social creatures, we are held to this planet by a social glue — our commitments to family and friends. Our happiness depends on how well we can negotiate our style, values, attitudes and beliefs within the social network rather than opting for isolation. For this reason, the social learning that takes place outside the classroom has no parallel and is indispensable in a society geared to age differentiation, competition and cooperation.

So seriously do I view the role of the playground in kids' welfare that I challenge every school to really examine what it is doing by way of social skills development training and social skills remediation. Kids can get by in life without being a good reader, or speller, or writer, or mathematician, but it's purgatory if they're not good at getting on with other humans. I'm aware that many schools are addressing this issue as a high priority with special programs and special staff allocation.

This chapter looks at the problems kids face outside the classroom, in virtually any playground environment, regardless of how carefully selected that environment may be. It looks at the shy kids, the lonely kids, the bullies and the victims, the sensitive kids, the rejected kids, even kids who don't eat a decent lunch or won't front up for their lunchtime medication. I've tried to avoid home-based problems (defiance, swearing, non-cooperation, fighting, etc.), and parents concerned about these problems would enjoy reading my books *Who'd Be a Parent?: The Manual That Should Have Come With the Kids* and/or *Coping With the Family*.

Shy kids

Of all the mistakes we make in parenting, nothing quite compares to the mess we make of shy kids. We know that the fear, the embarrassment and the anxiety that goes into this phobia about other people is the worst feeling on Earth, yet how do we help our kids through this burning, shrivelling fear of the social spotlight? As the kids hide from the spotlight, we say cute little things like, 'Don't be shy, tell the man your name!' Not only does labelling them as shy guarantee a lifelong problem but, even worse, for a shy kid telling their name is like psychologically streaking in public. In fact, so difficult and embarrassing is self-naming that some cultures ban it altogether!

For young kids meeting new people is perhaps the biggest fear of all. However, research done with teenagers by Philip Zimbardo and a team at the Stanford University Shyness Clinic (that's probably why you've never heard of it), puts talking in front of a large group as the worst fear for that age group. This is followed by facing situations in which the kids feel inferior, or in which they are being judged or required to be assertive, or those in which they are controlled by anything new, or when they are feeling vulnerable, especially one-to-one meetings with the opposite sex. Regardless of the situation the symptoms are fairly similar. An overwhelming need to conform, timidity, embarrassment, a soft voice and quietness are the most common forms of behaviour, although some can mask it fairly well. Not every shy kid is introverted or withdrawn — some, in fact, can appear quite extroverted and will use clowning or drama/acting to hide their shyness and sense of panic.

Often it's our lack of belief in our kids that frequently contributes to their shyness. Over-protection, for instance, signals to kids that they can't cope, so they never learn to trust themselves; they become caught in cotton wool that cocoons them like a straitjacket. Others have suffered under constant criticism or comparison with more outgoing or successful brothers and sisters. But it's also true that some shy kids may be copying shy parents and, even more to the point, there are strong suggestions that in many kids there are shy genes at work.

How to help

- Respect the child's right to be reserved; not to be put on exhibition or compared with other people, especially siblings; and to set their own time limit on relating to others.

- Try to remember your own or someone else's difficulties with shyness. Perhaps you could tell one or two of your own funny 'shy-type' experiences: describe how you felt, what you did, and how you overcame the particular problem. By sharing the experiences you not only let the kids see you warts and all, but also help them to realise that they're not alone in having these feelings, and that they can be overcome.
- Take the confidence-building process in small steps, starting with what they have already conquered, and sharing ideas about what they could conquer next — like saying hello, saying a name, saying something nice, listening hard or joining in. After they've faced a challenge, share their joy if it was successful or, if it wasn't, work on a new plan with even smaller steps so they can't help but get that winning feeling. Don't push the pace.
- Resist the temptation to take over. Have confidence and your kids will develop their own! Resist the impulse to protect; you can't always be there.
- Give them the chance to build confidence on their own — choosing clothes to wear and colours that make them feel good; sure, they might mess it up at first but it's better on the outside than on the psyche. Going on a camp or excursion or to sport with other kids, without parents being around, gives them the chance to find their feet so they don't get tangled up around yours.
- Make a game of shifting the 'I'm no good' talk to 'I can do it' talk, such as 'I will count how many people I can say hello to at this party'— and let your kids practise new things. Maybe they can even practise a nice, easy phrase or two before an event; some kids practise in front of the mirror, using kids' names, what they'll say, what they'll comment on (hair, dress, etc.).
- Touch, trust and tenderness are the foundations of good

psychological health, so work on those areas rather than addressing the child's shyness as your overall aim.

- Don't treat your children as exhibits to be shown off — or they'll really demonstrate what an exhibition is all about.
- When you have visitors don't force the pace. Don't focus on the kids at all until they have had a chance to adjust to another 'genial giant'. Give them time and within 10 minutes you'll find they are ready to make an approach. To draw them in, it frequently works to use an incidental approach, like asking their opinion on a product in a magazine or which team they barrack for in the footie.
- The big message is never label your kids as 'shy'. Sticks and stones may break our bones but labels last forever.
- Shyness often develops from a sense of not being able to live up to or deliver what is expected of us. So it's worth checking to see if we are imposing our personal agendas on our kids' personalities. Sometimes I find that kids act shy when parents are overpowering — these kids present as shy, but their feelings are often swallowed or repressed anger.
- If the kids are a bit older and starting to worry about shyness, let them find their own strengths to help them gain self-confidence. Some kids improve with the confidence-building techniques of a martial arts program such as Zen Bu Kan; others at drama groups; still others gain benefit from deportment classes; and, of course, sport is the great socialiser and keeps relationships activity- rather than personality-based. Some shy kids really take to computers, Internet and chat sites because they find the interactions much less threatening. While these may not be our ideal, for really shy kids it may be their first step to self-confidence and meeting up with like-minded individuals.
- Some kids choose to use little techniques to mask the difficulty they have with making eye contact, such as

103

wearing dark glasses, talking to their hands or looking at someone's lips rather than their eyes. Many shy people find it easier to put an extra metre between them and the other person as a psychological safety zone, so let them learn to find their easy distance in conversations.

- As shyness is a social problem, in many ways it has to be solved in a social arena; all the talking and pleading from parents has little transfer to the kids' day-to-day situation. Let the teacher know of your concern and ask what program or opportunities they're working on to develop social confidence; this might mean getting shy kids up as part of a group rather than on their own to do class presentations, involving them in a drama production with set lines and a different character to their own, capitalising on their talent (e.g. drawing, Web searching) to give them status and a secure role in a group project, etc.

Many schools are now instigating social skills programs to help kids who are experiencing social problems. Programs commonly being used include the following:

- Room 14 Social Language Program (Silvereye)
- Tough Kids Social Skills Program (Silvereye)
- Social Skills and Anger Management Course (Dominie)
- Friendly Kids, Friendly Classrooms (Longmans).

Tips from teachers

✐ Teachers generally favoured the idea of getting the kids involved in sport or some group such as Brownies or Cubs, but many found that inviting school playmates over after school was very successful.

✐ 'Be prepared for them to try various activities until they find what suits their style because many shy children just don't believe they are good at anything.'

✐ 'Let them play alongside other children without pushing for full participation.'

✐ 'It's just their personality and it will take many years (believe me) to stop feeling shy.'

✐ 'Encourage their independence and don't allow them to use you as their shy cover all the time.'

Lonely kids

Shyness and loneliness often go hand in hand, so read through the section above if your kids are lonely. Chronic loneliness for kids is absolutely demoralising — they've lost the measuring stick that tells them they are okay and that they are somebody! But sometimes the things we do make them feel like nobodies. This includes being overcritical so they feel they're not good enough, making the kids so 'unique' or different that other kids see them as weird, shifting school too often for them to develop friendships, etc.

Kids who have no friends or can't make friends are deprived of much of the social experience of being human; no wonder they are invariably such sad characters.

Loneliness checklist

Your child may be suffering from loneliness if they:

- do not want to go to school
- watch lots of television
- want money to buy things for friends

- live in the school library every lunchtime
- mention different names each time you ask about friends
- never receive phone calls or invitations
- are a bossy-boots at play

How to help
- Get the kids off to a flying start by letting them mix with other kids from a very early age.
- Make sure your house has a decent play area or visit local playgrounds that can be used as a play area or meeting spot.
- If you have decided to live out of town then you have to accept that you will be offering a free taxi and motel service.
- Help the kids to build skills and interests or to join clubs (like Cubs and Brownies) that give them something to share with other kids.

But the secret to beating loneliness is not just to have something to share, it's knowing how to share it. And how do kids learn that? Simply by sharing a friendship with us, by watching us share, watching how we handle friends and how we handle disagreements. If this takes time and effort, so what? If we can leave our children with the ability to make friends, then that's got to be about the best legacy that any parent can offer.

Questions and answers

Q   My son keeps coming home from school saying he has no one to play with. I feel so sorry for him but what can I do?

1. Don't take over. We've all had to weather some tough times and we are the better for it. Just express your confidence in his ability to beat his problem. Don't promote dependence.
2. Really listen to what he's saying and then reflect what you think he's feeling (sad, angry, etc.) rather

106

than focusing on the content. This keeps you in touch and conveys to him that you care.

3. Help him problem-solve a few ways out of his loneliness — for example, what he could do to get the kids to play with him.

4. Set a time limit of, say, a week to check how well the plan is working.

5. If the plan is proceeding well, then refine it; if not, set up some new tactics or perhaps talk to someone like your son's teacher or counsellor, not only for ideas but to find out what's going wrong.

Q   My son sometimes plays well with other kids, but often he says he just wants to play cars or do something on his own. Should I be worried?

Some kids are simply self-sufficient and don't appear to need friends as much as other people do. As long as they know how to mix, how to share, how to work with others, and how to enjoy fun with others, then I don't think they have a problem, particularly if all the other indicators show they are pretty happy and well adjusted.

Q   I know I shouldn't pick my child's friends, but I really get worried about some of the dreadful kids she is mixing with. I've heard some terrible stories. What should I do?

1. Like it or not you can't pick your children's friends, and if you try to unpick friendships it frequently makes a child more determined to keep them.

2. Try not to make your daughter choose between friends and family. Sometimes I've had success through a role reversal — when 'friends' have done

something nasty to her, ask her would a friend do that, would she do that, to someone she liked. Sometimes this will alert her to the fact that she is putting more into the friendship than they are.
3. If she says her friends are good, then use logical consequences — if they're good for you then I'm sure they'll make you feel good and act 'good'. If that's not happening then it throws the problem into stark relief.
4. Maybe get the 'bad' friends over to get to know them. They may be better than you think, and they may get better if they like the contact with you.
5. Have confidence that your basic training will win out in the long run, and remember that all kids have to learn through trial and (hopefully only a little) error.

Solution summary

- **F**-ind their strengths
- **R**-eassure your child that everyone is looking for friends
- **I**-nstil your confidence in their ability to find a friend
- **E**-ncourage positive attempts to make friends
- **N**-ever take over, buy friends or publicise your child's problem
- **D**-iscourage self-pity and encourage action to meet other kids
- **S**-hare your own similar experiences and positive outcomes
- **H**-ave a talk to the teacher to work on class activities to enhance friendships
- **I**-nvite friends with similar aged kids for a day out
- **P**-raise any success
- **S**-top any home hindrances (e.g. overprotection, overindulgence)

CASE STUDY

Tony

Why Tony would want to make an attempt on his own life would be beyond the imagination of the average outsider. Tony had a good home, a good brain, good gear, was a top tennis player — in fact, Tony had everything, except friends. His parents thought being the best would win him best friends but he was just too competitive and too big-headed for the other kids, who would tease him terribly, scrunch his hat, hurl his bag, anything to make his life miserable. His parents told the teacher who told the class to go easy on Tony — and that made things worse because it signalled he was weak. And it was no good telling him to steer clear of the kids giving him a hard time because he desperately wanted to be their friend.

So Tony and I talked about the sort of kid who would be their friend and he decided he wanted to have a go. That meant being stronger in body and mind, someone who could share and someone who made others feel good, not always trying to be better than everybody. So away he went — he started Zen Bu Kan to give him confidence, started making a habit of not big-noting himself and then, to his credit, suddenly decided to front the kids direct with a challenge: 'If I could prove to you that I can take it would you be more friendly to me?'

News is that he's doing well, gaining confidence and that means gaining friends.

Kids' comments

- Instead of using teacher tips here, I asked the kids all about loneliness. I think you'll find their comments sobering.
- 'You get lonely when you don't have friends or there's no one to talk to or you're left out'.
- 'I think kids don't want to play with me because of the way I look'.

109

> - 'When my mum or dad think I've been bad they send me to my room for a long time and that is a very lonely place to be when you're sad'.
> - 'When I have a fight or I don't fit in then I feel very very lonely.
> - When my cat died was the loneliest time for me ever'.
> - 'I never feel lonely because I've always got myself'.
> - 'I think most 12-year-olds feel lonely when they've broken up with their boyfriend'.
> - 'I felt all alone when my mum left on her honeymoon and we weren't allowed to go'.
> - 'When I changed school was the worst'.
> - 'When I fell over and Mummy wasn't there'.
> - 'When my two friends go off and leave me with no one'.
> - 'When I'm grounded it is very lonely'.
> - 'If I'm left out of a party it is bad enough, if I'm not invited I feel even worse'.
> - 'When somebody you know does something bad to you and you don't think you can tell anybody'.
> - When a friend backstabs me'.
> - 'If you have different coloured skin you always feel lonely'.
> - 'If your parents are getting divorced you feel really lonely because you don't know which one you will live with and then you will miss the other one'.
> - 'When my parents fight and talk about divorce I just want to cry and feel like I wish that I had never been born'.

Kids with low self-esteem

You can throw in your Pokémons, Nintendos, Tazos, Play Stations, weeps-as-she-wees-as-she-walks dolls, rollers, remote control cars and all the other technology designed for kids today, but everything pales beside the happiness that children get from the feeling that they are esteemed or valued people. Without self-esteem or self-respect kids become emotional paupers begging for handouts and hating the scraps. So how do your kids rate on this quiz? (Give 2 points for 'yes', 1 point for 'sometimes', and 0 for 'no'.)

1. Do they make friends easily?
2. Are they active and happy most of the time?
3. Are they happy with the way they look?
4. Can they tolerate frustration?
5. Can they make decisions easily?
6. Do they have energy in the morning?
7. Are they interested in new things and take initiative?
8. Are they confident in tackling day-to-day tasks?

If the score was really low, then so is the kid's self-esteem. But before you start a guilt trip, let me tell you that the whole area of self-esteem is riddled with contradictions. What parents and teachers often do to enhance self-esteem may not have that effect. Recent research in America found that many bullies and criminals had high self-esteem and many high school girls who were high achievers didn't! I don't know if you're aware of it but at the moment there's a big backlash against the 1970s–1980s 'self-esteem movement' in schools. The 'old school' says there's no evidence that the self-esteem school has produced any less violence or any better academic results — so, they say, let's get back to basics.

Both the self-esteem movement and the back-to-basics movement have missed the point — you can't give empty praise to kids, telling them they're good if they're not! That's just ego-tripping. On the other hand, you can't go just back to basics either, as that doesn't prepare children with the skills or attitudes to cope in a computer-, commuter-, communication-driven community.

What is needed is a bit of common sense. What we're doing is confusing self-worth with self-esteem. The way to help kids sense that they're valued and have worth comes not from giving them empty praise, nor from defining worth in just a few narrow academic subjects and ignoring the other types of intelligence that are important in life — social skills, music, aesthetic, sport, art, common sense. A real sense of worth comes from knowing others like and value you. That feeling of being liked starts at home; telling kids they're valued but never finding time to be with them or wanting to listen to them or share or laugh together gives them a very mixed message — and kids are quick to pick up on hypocrisy. So if you want your kids to feel good enough to tackle their weaknesses, and to feel good enough without fearing failure all the time, then give them no empty praise, no tight definition of worth in terms of how many they're beating in the classroom or playground — just show them they're valued by the fact that you value your time with them.

However, while parents may be the first and most important source of self-esteem, once kids get to primary school they start to be more concerned about what other kids think of them. At this stage a struggling kid may be getting every reassurance in the world from Mum and Dad, but if the peer group doesn't think they're good value then our kids won't value themselves highly, that is, they develop low 'self-esteem'. I often feel that kids low in self-esteem have lost something they value — time with parents, respect from peers, confidence in their own ability, feeling of physical well-being, etc. In other words we need to work on the causes, not the presenting symptom.

How to help
Many ideas are listed below because it's such an important area. But none of them will make the slightest difference if the basic building block is missing — family (and school) not just talking self-esteem but showing by their priorities that they really value the kids. It's a child's worth to others that determines their sense of self-worth.

1.   Find what they love doing — the things you can see from their eyes and faces that really give them a lift. If you don't know, go down the list below and see if any spark their interest or, better still, spark a joint interest between parent and child. For a low self-esteem boy, sharing and getting on well with Dad (or some special adult male) may be the single biggest boost he can get!

Children's interest inventory

acting
aeroplanes
aquariums
art

astronomy
balloons
Barbies
baseball
baseball cards
bike riding
bird watching
board games
boats
bush walks
card games
carpentry
cars and trucks
chemistry
clay modelling
climbing
clock collecting
clothes (dressing up)
coin collecting
colouring in
computers
cooking
cricket
cubbies
dancing
dinosaurs
dolls
drawing

electricity
electronics
fishing
football

gardening
geography
handyman jobs
hair brushing
hiking
history
insects
Internet
kites
Lego blocks
lizards
magic
magnets
make believe
make-up
map reading
marbles
martial arts
mechanics
microscopes
miniature soldiers
model making
money making
movies
music
pet care
photography
Pokémon

poetry
puppets
puzzles
radio and crystal
sets
reading books
remote control cars
rollerblading
running
science fiction
Scouts and Guides
seashell collecting
sewing
singing
skateboarding
skating
soccer
stamp collecting
storms
story telling
stuffed animals
swimming
T-ball
telephoning
television
telling jokes
travelling
video games
water
weather forecasting
writing stories
yo-yos
yo-yo diablo

Use this interest inventory to see which ones inspire —
where parent and child interests coincide will be the
source of family fun as well as a sense of self-worth.
If they're obscure or uncommon interests then phone

Community Information Services for a local contact. If their sense of self-worth is so low they can't even make the effort, and if you have some good contacts around town, see if you can orchestrate a 'surprise' phone call or visit. If parents suggest something it's probably doomed to rejection, but if the offer comes from outside, it tells them that they really are wanted.

2. Focus on success, even though the kids want to focus on failure. One way to do that is by reframing their problem. For instance, if the kids say that everyone hates them: start by challenging the fact that all the kids feel that way

   • see if they can identify any that don't hate them, which ones spoke to them, what their friends might like about them (e.g. being kind, doesn't cheat, shares games, doesn't try to go first all the time)

   • then work out ways they can get the kids to see these talents and watch the reaction they get

   • that night talk about the tactics they used, how it went and what they'll do the next day to build bridges to friendship.

3. Challenge the kids to identify any habits they have that might not go over well. Then see if they're ready to do some habit busting, what different behaviour they'll try to do instead and report back the next night on how it went.

4. Teach positive self-talk skills if your child is using negatives on herself/himself ('I'm stupid', 'I'm ugly', 'nobody likes me'). Some use challenges such as, 'Am I stupid or is the person picking on me stupid?' or 'What if they do think I'm an idiot, so is Bart Simpson, and see how many people love him!'

5. Do find areas where they can achieve at school even if they're not brilliant at schoolwork — art, sport, kindness, craft, projects, computers, board cleaner-upper. Kids need endorsement from the fact that they have something to offer before they can feel good about themselves.

6.   Do try to find time to have a success-sharing time every night so everyone can talk about one success or good thing that day.

7.   Keep a scrapbook for each of the kids with all awards, memorabilia, and anything else that makes them feel good.

8.   If the kids can read, think about instigating the Magic Macaroni Tin! This tin is a special jar, left beside the child's bed. When family or close friends stay over, get them to write on a thin slip of paper one thing they like about the child (kind to people, lovely grin, always makes them feel special, a big helper, hard worker, etc.). Each thought is placed inside a different piece of macaroni so when the kids are down they go to their Magic Macaroni Tin, unravel a few, read the message and get the lift and the memory to shift their mood.

9.   Talk to the teacher about things that can be done at school to boost their feelings of worth. For example, each Infants child takes a turn in the middle of the room to be bombarded with positive statements (things other kids like/respect about each other). With older kids it's often less embarrassing if they write them out anonymously, put them in a hat or container and then hand them across to the child in focus.

CASE STUDY

Barry

Barry's mum told me he was a blob. She was sick of him soiling, not being able to do anything, and playing up when she had a friend to stay. The first time I met them she ranted and raved about Barry while the 7-year-old just sat there and I waited to get a word in. No, she said, she couldn't tell me one good thing about him.

We owe it to our kids to be their advocates. If they can't count on their parents, where do they go? So we tried a 10:1 scheme. Barry's mum could say only one negative thing for every 10 positive ones. 'What a lovely smile, Barry', 'Thanks for setting the table'... She had trouble finding two positive things, let alone 10, and constantly had to restrain herself from verbally abusing him. But, you know, Barry stopped soiling, started smiling, began to work and wanted to please — all because he began to feel that he was wanted.

Tips from teachers

✍ Teachers were fairly united in saying that the best way parents could build on a child's sense of self-worth was to find the positive things they could do, to build on those and when the child made mistakes to focus on fixing the behaviour rather than blaming the child.

✍ 'One parent once gave me these words of wisdom: "Often the difference between a good and bad school day is 5 minutes of a parent's time".'

Discrimination — bullies and victims

Discrimination

Every school now has to have a policy on discrimination, which is defined as any form of victimisation (culture, race, language, age, sex, intellectual, or socioeconomic) either direct or indirect. While bullying may be the most obvious and attention-grabbing aspect of discrimination, it can take many forms: physical (blows, kicks, pushing); gestural (intimidating or threatening actions and gestures); verbal (name calling and abusive comments); indirect (deliberately not including someone or removing their belongings, etc.); relational (setting up others to hurt or ostracise someone).

Bullying

Nothing undermines our task of helping kids thrive at school more than the disastrous and soul-destroying impact of bullying. Of course kids have to learn how to cope with the good, the bad and the ugly — that's life. But it seems that bullying is on the increase. Bureau of Crime statistics indicate that the number of reported school assaults has more than doubled since 1995. Weapons were used in approximately 10 per cent of these assaults, most attacks occurred at lunchtime and there were several cases of children as young as 6 years of age being assaulted.

No doubt increased reporting has much to do with the statistical shift and no doubt the decision that every school must have its own anti-bullying policy will assist in addressing the problem.

While there are no precise figures on the numbers of juvenile bullies, teachers often quote the figure of 15 per cent as their best guess-timate, that's about 3 per average class, and that's a lot of terror for some kids. A Norwegian study in 1990 found four factors help to create a bully: lack of time and interest from the bully's parents in his early years, a highly aggressive and dominant personality, too much tolerance towards his aggressive behaviour and use of physical punishment.

What this boils down to is that the bullies see that their behaviour works, they are allowed to get away with it and they have had the same tactics used on them. Worse still, the study found that 60 per cent of untreated bullies went on to receive at least one serious criminal conviction.

More recent research has found that most Conduct Disordered children were engaging in bullying behaviour before the age of 6 years! So intervention needs to happen at the first signs of behaviour that seeks to deliberately and repeatedly humiliate or hurt other children. Treatment can be effective; even at age 18 success rates appear to be better than 50 per cent. Research in Norway is also reporting real success when parents and teachers work together with common attitudes and a zero tolerance outlook. This includes an absolute insistence on decent behaviour, backed up by non-physical punishments such as no television, sport, transport, pocket money or whatever pleasures parents have control over. Some techniques instigated by schools include the following:

- Channelling kids into areas of achievement and physical challenge — sport, bushwalking, abseiling, farming, orienteering, etc. (I find this at times extremely successful — tough kids being challenged by tough nature and bonding in the process.)
- Programs giving kids skills in conflict resolution.
- Programs where the bully works with young kids or animals to not only occupy them but to highlight their protective potential.
- Programs where the bully is buddied-up to a popular high-flier in the school to copy their style and to gain contact with good kids. (I've found this works for a while but wears thin for both the good kids and the bullies.)
- An increasingly popular technique, now being taken up by magistrates in Children's Courts, is to have the bully meet with the victim and family and cooperatively decide on ways in which the bully can repay the victim in some agreed way.

CASE STUDY
Luke

Luke was a fighter. At the age of 7 he could flatten any kid in the Infants school, but the more he hit, the more he was hated, and the more heated he became. His language was foul, his friends were few and school was fed up — they were ready to kick him out.

Everyone's recipe for curing him failed — the school tried detention; the family tried deprivation; but no one tried inspiration. Luke's world was just as negative about him as he was about it.

So Mum began to create a different world around him. She used television time to gain cooperation in family chores, with the further incentive of giving him a choice of jobs; his dad tied a fishing trip to a good weekly report from school; the teacher linked spending lunchtime with the other kids to a 'hit-free' day—otherwise he would be sent to the office; and we arranged for him to learn Zen Bu Kan to smarten up his self-control.

A while back Luke brought in his chart and photo album bursting with merit certificates for good behaviour. His mum reckons that the first hint of success made him hungry for more, and then the whole positive approach just snowballed.

Victims

Some kids live in enormous fear of bullies — it can be so bad that they lose sleep, appetite and health and become depressed. Others act out their pain by becoming bullies themselves. If your kid is always the victim, then the chances are that they need to learn how to avoid contact with bullies, how to assert the message for the bully to 'back off' if they are confronted, how to stop aggravating the bullies and, as a back-up, maybe some self-defence tactics — but be warned: advertised skills attract challengers. Whatever the tactics, the message must be that bullying is not acceptable.

How to help

- Good strategies for victims include the following:
  - Examining their own behaviour to make sure that they ooze confidence and don't cower like a victim or stir other kids.
  - Controlling their own fear so they're not so easily intimidated—this can be done, for instance, by counting the number of times the bully tries to upset them in word or deed, with the goal that by counting rather than reacting the daily score will go down because the taunt is being wasted.
  - Telling someone in authority and not being put off by a bully's threats to 'get' them if they dob — bullying is a form of assault.

119

- Calling the bully's bluff by telling them why they think the bully is bothering them.
- Exposing the jugular — acknowledging that the bully could beat them in a fight and, in so doing, taking the combat incentive away.
- Depriving the bully of opportunity — for instance, if the bully is taking their lunch money, bring lunch from home with no money.
- Reducing points of contact — playing in places and going places where they know the bully does not hang out.
- Networking — finding someone older and respected by the bully to act as friend and protector — but not as bodyguard.
- Making friends — many bullies are unhappy and offering friendship can sometimes be a way to settle the problem.

Developing assertiveness skills
There are several assertive techniques that my colleague Peter Clarke uses to help kids effectively use assertion. Select the style that suits your child's personality and circumstances.

Fogging
This technique involves kids using words to combat bullying. The words are designed to direct the bully's attention away from what is happening. For instance, if a bully keeps taking another child's pencilcase from the desk, the victim might say, 'I'm so glad you like my pencil case, why don't you buy one the same?'

Deflation
I like this technique, because many victims have told me how well it works. If you can raise the victims' self-esteem and self-image enough for them to realise that it's the bully that has the problem (that may require professional help) then they can be armed with a repertoire of standard phrases to deflate a verbal

insult attack. That could include just agreeing with the bully, or using phrases such as 'whatever you reckon', 'you're probably right', and then moving away from the scene.

Teasing tossing tactics

My favourite technique (see also 'Teasing' and other ideas in my book *Who'd Be a Parent?: The Manual That Should Have Come With the Kids*) is to get victims to tell me all the names they're being called that hurt them ('fatso', 'idiot', 'lame-brain', 'dick-head', etc.). Then I practice pushing them, giggling at them and calling them those names and they have to count (aloud) how many times I've tried to hurt by word or action. When they have the score correct then we practice counting silently. When that is working well, I set them loose to sidle up alongside a bully to give them a chance to practice the technique. When they get home they put the total for the day on the calendar. I'm so confident of the tactic, providing the victim is mentally set and eager to play the game, that I guarantee their bullying score will be near zero within 3 weeks. If they feel no one likes them I might use the variation of counting how many kids are nice to them and how many nice things they say to others and startle them with the change over the 3-week period.

Escalated assertion

If the bullying is particularly vicious and focused, this technique may be used. It involves raising the voice and explaining the worst consequences of the bully's action if it's going on and on. For example, if a bully keeps pestering another student by repeatedly hitting them or throwing things at them, the victim can at first simply say, 'Get lost'. If it's still happening the next level of response might be, 'Your choice, either get lost or get into trouble' and then move away. If it continues then the victim carries out their proposed course of action.

'I' statements

This technique involves the student saying how they feel about the bullying. For example, in response to a bully pushing in front of the queue at the canteen, the student could say, 'I was here first. I would like you to move to the end of the line'.

Three-part assertion

This technique involves stating the behaviour of the bully, telling the bully how the student is feeling, and telling the bully what effects have been created by their behaviour. It involves using the words, 'When you *behaviour* I feel *feeling*, because *effects*'. For example, if a bully keeps taking a ball away from a group playing handball, one of the victims might say, 'When you take the ball, we really feel pissed off and we don't want to play with you'.

Demanding responsibility

This technique is used in conjunction with some of the other techniques and involves the victim asking the bully to correct their behaviour. For example, the books give an example like this: 'You're harassing me and it's not right. I demand that you stop and apologise.' In everyday terms the kids are more likely to use, it converts to something like this, 'You're bugging me and I've had enough. Get lost and get a life.'

CASE STUDY

Sam

Some of the saddest kids I see are the targets of teasing, like 10-year-old Sam. The older kids at school had been calling him names and would take away his handball unless he told them how great they were, did up their shoelaces or kissed their feet.

In Sam's case we used a multi-pronged strategy to beat the problem:

- I supplied him with a few cartons of second-hand tennis balls. Sam now had the confidence to know that if he lost one there were more at home, so he had no need to panic.

- I taught him to use the teasing tossing tactics described on page 121.
- We decided that if the teasing was becoming too hot to handle, he would casually move the game closer to the playground teacher so that the 'stirrers' would be less comfortable about overt victimisation.
- Sam carried out his plan, and within 3 days all the harassment had stopped.

Tips from teachers

✐ Teachers consistently suggested that parents let the teacher or principal know — if it's happening at school or to and from school then the teacher wants to know about it. Teachers can be very subtle about helping out the situation without letting the bully know who dobbed.

✐ 'I'm a school principal and I've just been hearing on talkback radio a mother blaming the schools for not protecting her child from bullies. She said that she has now been to 6 schools, public and private, and they're all the same. Sometimes parents have a different social agenda to schools — they expect different things — so unless the parents and principal sit down and get common ground, not only will each be disappointed by the other but the child becomes the big loser and may never recover.'

✐ 'Never, never, do nothing. It will not go away.'

Sex play and child protection

Kids learn by playing, asking, exploring and copying. And kids will explore sex. Sometimes it will be in the guise of 'mothers and fathers', sometimes 'nurses and doctors', or the more up-market version, 'paramedic and patient'. The good news is that the aim is not sex so there's no need to call in welfare or worry about their welfare.

Behaviour checklist

- If it's just giggle, giggle, 'show me yours, I'll show you mine' type behaviour then that's kids getting to know which sex they are and what differences there are. I can't help but think of the story of a Kinder boy and girl coming out of their first sex education lesson. The little boy turns to the girl and says, 'Are you the opposite sex or am I?'

- If it's just grabbing at each other's genitals then that too is normal play, particularly for boys. Just a quiet talk about who's allowed to touch who, where, will probably be all that's needed. It could be that you have to start a habit-busting chart. Maybe even some countermove; if they start pulling at each other then they may have to keep their hands to themselves, say in their pockets. On second thoughts — not in their pockets, on their heads — till they reckon they'll be able to remember.

DO

✓   Do make your rules clear. If it's just normal play then just clear up your rules, no closed doors, teach 'good touch/bad

touch' and see if things settle. Try not to build shame into it. We want kids to feel good about their bodies.

✓ **Do** make sure you have plenty of close, comfy contact so the kids don't have to use sex play to get cuddles, and maybe keep their play out in the open.

✓ **Do** teach kids all about good touch and bad touch. Some parents practise tickling the kids, for example, to the point where it becomes unpleasant, so they can practise saying, 'Please don't do that any more', or a simple 'No!', easily and confidently. This type of exercise provides opportunities to talk about which parts of the body are okay to touch and which parts are private.

✓ **Do** consider reverse psychology. Sometimes with little boys who keep pulling at each other, I might do some 'flooding'. I suggest that I know they like to pull at their penis, but it's private. So they're welcome to go into their room and pull theirs as much as they like where no one else has to see them. In my clinic experience I've yet to see any evidence of a penis-puller going blind!

✓ **Do** handle kids' questions as openly and honestly as you can when they arise. If they are old enough to ask the question, then they are old enough to deserve an answer. If you're not sure what to say, pick up a copy of the pamphlet *What shall we tell the children?* from a Family Planning Clinic or its equivalent. If kids use obscene words tell them the correct word. If you're not sure get hold of a book such as Gill Mullinar's *Not Just Four-Letter Words: A Sex Dictionary for Today's Young People*.

DON'T

✗ **Don't** *assume* the worst. But if your child has been penis-sucking, fingering, or any other adult activity, chances are they've been exposed to some bad influence and/or sexually abused. Call the local sexual assault counsellor through your area health service, give them the details and ask their advice.

- You may be advised to just have a chat to the parent of the other child involved, not as an accusation, but just to compare notes and help to trace the source.
- You may also be advised to have a private little chat with your own child. But be careful, if you do, not to load your question (e.g. 'Did Uncle Pedo teach you to do that?'). Kids are extremely suggestible, and will latch on all too fast to what they think you want them to say. Say something like, 'Let's talk about what you were doing in your game ... Where did you learn to do that?'
- If either child nominates some adult or other child as the culprit, then please, no accusations, again talk to your sexual assault counsellor first.

Child protection

It's sad to think that this area has to be included in this edition because the number of cases are on the rise. The statistics reveal that 1 in 4 girls and 1 in 8 boys will be sexually abused before the age of 18. The continuing annual rise in physical abuse and the obviously increasing concern about child neglect in the community, have made this area impossible not to address. But for those parents worried about the sexual behaviour of their children, bear in mind that most of it is normal growing curiosity. Keep in mind, too, that 90 per cent of abuse is by a family member or someone well known to the child — lurking pedophiles are rarely the problem. And keep in mind that neglect and emotional abuse cases are much higher in incidence and often overlooked in our obsession with matters sexual.

Teachers and carers in all States are required to notify any suspected cases of abuse or neglect. They have identification criteria and procedures to follow so parents can be reassured that their child has a level of protection not previously afforded to kids. Here are some general indicators of abuse and neglect.

Indicators of possible neglect
- Poor standards of hygiene
- Scavenging or stealing food
- Extended stays at school, public places or other people's homes
- Extreme longing for adult affection
- A flat and superficial way of relating that lacks genuine warmth
- Anxiety about being dropped or abandoned
- Self-comforting behaviours — e.g. rocking or sucking
- Delays in developmental milestones
- Loss of skin bloom
- Poor hair texture
- Untreated physical problems

Indicators of possible emotional abuse
- Feelings of worthlessness about life and themselves
- Inability to value others
- Lack of trust in people and expectations
- Lack of the interpersonal skills necessary for adequate functioning
- Extreme attention-seeking behaviour
- Other behaviour disorders such as disruptiveness, aggressiveness or bullying

Indicators of possible physical abuse
- Facial, head and neck bruising and other injuries
- Lacerations and welts from excessive discipline or physical restraint
- Explanation offered by the child is inconsistent with the injury
- Other marks or bruising that may show the shape of the object (e.g. hand prints, buckle marks)
- Bite marks and scratches
- Multiple injuries or bruises
- Ingestion of alcohol, harmful drugs or other poisonous

substances
- Dislocations, sprains and twisting
- Burns and scalds

Indicators of possible sexual abuse
- Describing sexual acts
- Disclosures, direct or indirect
- Age-inappropriate sexual behaviour
- Self-destructive behaviour
- Sexual themes in art work, play or writing
- Persistent running away from home
- Anorexia or overeating
- Going to bed fully clothed
- Regression to more babyish or immature behaviour
- Child being in contact with known or suspected perpetrator
- Unexplained accumulation of money or gifts
- Bleeding from the vagina, anus or external genitalia
- Injuries such as tears or bruising to genitalia or anus
- Sexually transmitted diseases
- Injuries to breasts, buttocks, lower abdomen and thighs
- Teenage pregnancy

These are all heavy-action criteria but I thought that by listing them parents may be more attuned to what it's all about and also be sensitive if they feel other children in their community may be abused or neglected

What to do
- Talk to your kids about self-protection, not to make them scared of every adult they meet, but how to play it safe — such as playing in safe areas, not walking alone along the road or through parks, etc., and developing an inner sixth sense. For example:
  - being aware if someone is invading their personal space

- listening to their inner feelings if someone is somehow making them feel uncomfortable, in what they say or do, how they touch, etc.
- doing the '5-finger test' of 5 people they trust that they can talk to if they're worried or who they can tell private/secret things to if they need to
- knowing what to do or where to go if they feel scared
- being confident in telling someone to please stop if that person is doing or saying something that makes them feel uncomfortable.

- Few things cause more damage or rifts between families or within families than abuse! If you have any concerns talk to your doctor, clinic sister, school counsellor before assuming the worst — many of the symptoms outlined above, on their own may have nothing to do with abuse. Notifications must be on 'reasonable' grounds — many's the teacher who has been damned on somebody's hearsay.
- Be aware that community members may make anonymous notifications if they wish. Persons who notify suspected cases are protected by law from defamation and court appearance (but check State legislation in this regard — your school principal will know).
- Be aware that school teachers, counsellors and school principals in most States are legally obliged to notify any suspected cases, direct to police or the State children's welfare service — they do not have the discretion to decide the merits of the case.
- Parents are not advised to discuss the matter with the family of the child who is suspected of being abused or neglected; it must be discussed with professionals who have expertise in the area and who know the procedures to follow.
- As abuse and neglect cases can destroy lives and reputations, make sure of the facts, do not use hearsay

as evidence, and do not assume the worst just because one symptom is noticed.

✍ **Tips from teachers**

✍ 'Children are naturally sexually curious. Avoid opportunities for "secret" play and teach them about self-protection.'

✍ 'A little girl I taught was shying away from any adult affection. She later disclosed to me that her 15-year-old (soon to be) stepbrother was sexually abusing her. I notified Welfare who held an investigation. The mother refused to believe it all, married her man, and moved away interstate. I worry that it might still be going on and wonder if there was anything else I could have or should have done.'

Lunch problems

A neighbour loves sharing her problems with the rest of the street! 'Look what I found in your bag,' she told her son loud enough for us all to hear, 'your lunch! Don't worry that I got up at 6.30 to make it for you, you wanted peanut butter sandwiches and you got them. So? And it's not just today's lunch either, there's yesterday's and the day before's, your stinky bag will soon walk home on its own.'

It's understandable that parents should get stressed about school lunches, not just because of the wasted effort, but our society spends a lot of energy worrying about food intake, and well it might, given that dietitians tell us that 60 per cent of deaths are diet-related!

Lots of kids lose out on lunch — too busy, too hot, too many other things to do, lunch too boring. Some parents just let them buy it and keep some control by having their say on what the canteen stocks, others get the kids to make their own so they make what they'll eat and give the kids the money saved as extra pocket money, others deduct $2 for any food made but not eaten, perfect parents make lunches for the kids but keep the variety up with some little surprise from time to time.

Just remember that although 60 per cent of the population of our country may die of food-related problems, starvation is rarely the problem! So, work out lunch arrangements in ways that suit your values and the kids' needs and cause the least fuss — not like Daryl's family.

CASE STUDY
Daryl

Daryl was a fussy eater who particularly avoided his 'apple a day'. In frustration his father told him that every day he ate his apple, he would be given 20¢. Now Daryl soon figured out that he could get 20¢ just for dumping his apple in the bin. When one of his friends told on him, his parents decided they would pay by the scalp; Daryl would get 20¢ for each core he brought home. Being a boy of some ingenuity, Daryl worked out that he could still pocket 15¢ per apple by paying 5¢ to a fruit-loving friend to eat it for him.

When this game was discovered Daryl just stopped even pretending to eat the apples. In desperation his dad threatened to give him a swipe on the backside with his belt for every uneaten apple. A few weeks later, his father followed an alcoholic stench to 9 uneaten apples in Daryl's bag. Now he had to follow through on his threat.

Daryl is now 30 and still hasn't forgiven his dad for the thrashing — and he still can't eat red apples. His father still remembers crying with every swipe. If only:

- He hadn't tried to enforce something he couldn't police.

- He had consulted a nutrition chart which would have shown him that there were dozens of excellent alternatives to apples.

- He hadn't become obsessed with the idea that Daryl's survival hung on an apple tree.

- He hadn't made threats from which he either had to back off and look weak, or enforce and feel weak.

131

- He and his wife had taken a few notes on what Daryl really ate in a day — they would have found more variety and nutrition than most of us think our kids eat.

What to do

- Get to know your kids' favourite foods.
- Make sure their lunches have variety and, when possible, include a surprise.
- Talk to your child's teacher if the problem is serious; most schools supervise the first half of lunchtime and can keep kids who avoid eating their lunch nearby.
- Remember that everyone has different cycles; some can't eat much breakfast, some lunch, while others don't eat much dinner, so don't fuss if your child's appetite is not ideal.
- Restrict after-school eating if it is interfering excessively with your child's lunch or evening meal. Alternately, as kids' appetites tend to peak between 3 p.m. and 4 p.m., maybe allow healthy snack food after school, so when the worms get wistful, the kids can have their fill on good food. That takes the pressure off the evening meal as the sole provider for survival and means you can expect better behaviour and manners, or they leave the table. By the way, eating in front of TV every night is good neither for digestion nor for the family's emotional health and survival.
- If the kids will only eat junk food then chances are (from my experience) that they have some behaviour problems too. That's the only conclusion I can reach after reading Sue Dengate's book *Fed Up*, which looks at the link between problem behaviours in kids and the foods they eat. Sue Dengate claims that children who are irritable, restless, or inattentive, moody, poor sleepers, have eczema, migraines, headaches, stomach problems, bloating, diarrhoea, bedwetting, reflux, colic and asthma could well be reacting, at least in part, to

common foods. She goes further — in one study she quotes, of 140 people with behavioural symptoms, 74 per cent reacted to salicylates or the chemicals in some fruits, 67 per cent reacted to preservatives, 54 per cent reacted to food colouring, 41 per cent to antioxidants, 40 per cent to amines, and 39 per cent to MSG. Even if the case is overstated, we can't afford to underrate the issue. If the child has poor eating habits or cravings, see your family doctor who may refer them to a dietitian.

- If it's just a bad habit then take up some of these suggestions:
  - Cut junk food from the shopping list.
  - Maybe give afternoon commercial TV a miss as it's a heavy campaigner for junk food.
  - Keep plenty of healthy snack foods around, including fruit, nuts, muesli, yoghurt, carrot sticks, multigrain or high-fibre bread, etc.
  - Keep a list for a day or two of everything that is being eaten at home (and at school, if you know), not only to reassure yourself, but as valuable information for any future discussions with a dietitian, doctor or even with your child.

- Become involved in developing a good food policy at your school canteen. After consulting experts in the area, I have come to realise just how much a healthy canteen has to offer not just the kids but the whole school. Healthy-canteen advocates point out the following:
  - School canteens are the biggest takeaway food outlets in Australia, with a customer base of 1.2 million people and the potential to earn thousands of dollars for the school each year.
  - The workers constitute the biggest volunteer workforce in Australia.
  - School canteens have clear guidelines on the type of foods that the canteens are to sell to their students.

Programs such as 'Management Sense, Food Sense' provide a practical manual to assist canteen managers with information, recipe ideas, templates and computer disks to assist in all areas of canteen management.

- Healthy school canteens can be profitable — how profitable a canteen is depends on how efficiently it is run, not just on how healthy the food is.
- Many school canteens now offer healthy breakfasts as well as lunches because evidence suggests that children perform better in the classroom if they have had a healthy start to the day and don't skip breakfast.

Tips from teachers

✏ Generally the teachers were of the opinion that families should set a healthy example and only offer healthy food to kids.

✏ Other teachers suggested that we should worry less as kids will eat when they need to.

✏ 'So much of what children eat depends on the fads of their mates at school. Healthy canteens are becoming more prevalent and local area health services have brochures to assist your canteen with ideas to improve their fare.'

Medication problems

Medication of children is becoming a huge issue for society and a real problem for schools as more and more kids with more and more 'behavioural' disorders are being treated with medication. University estimates are that 1 in 5 children now suffer some form of mental distress with many being prescribed medication to be taken at school. Every school is faced with a new challenge in the new millennium: how to cooperate with the extent and variety of medication demands. Many schools now have a special 'Ritalin bell' when all children on medication go to the office to have their dose. Many school systems insist that any medication be held at the office, not only to ensure that it's taken, but also to prevent the medication falling into the wrong hands or being taken inappropriately. The problem for schools and even preschools is how to handle the legal drug pressures. The problem for kids taking medication is how to handle the social pressures, because they are perceived by the others to be different. For this reason, or for other personal reasons or hang-ups, some kids may avoid taking their prescription medication or only pretend that they have, and that can be as dangerous.

Many school systems around the country still leave it up to the family to oversee or rely on the goodwill and cooperation of individual teachers.

What to do

- The first step is to contact the school and find out the policy — don't just settle for rumour. This does not require a conference with the teacher — the school's office staff will be able to inform you of all you need to know and do or will give you a copy of the policy.
- Where a policy does exist it will probably contain these elements:
  - Where medication is required, parents may be asked, for the sake of the child and administration, to check with the doctor to see if the medication can be given outside school hours.
  - Where medication is to be taken during school hours, parents will be asked to clearly label it with the student's name, details of the medication and dosage, and the prescribing doctor's name.
  - Staff will be asked to compile a schedule for each child as to what medication is to be taken when.
  - Children will be informed as to the school's procedures for coming to the office or designated spot to receive their medication (generally avoiding peak periods so that the medicating can be monitored).
  - Medication will normally be kept in a central

location and parents will normally be asked to supply enough for just that day; this may be impractical for some medications, so parents would need to check this out.

- It will be the parents' responsibility to ensure that stocks of medication for their child are adequate and don't run out or expire.

- Regardless of the policy, it's important that you find time to either write to the teacher, or discuss with the teacher, early in the year, the implications of the medication — what it's for, when it's to be taken, consequences on behaviour of taking or not taking it, maybe even some of the signs that the medication may not have been taken.

- If, as is still occasionally the case, the school regards medication management as the pupil's own responsibility, then you will need to set up some very clear, concrete and consistent procedures or the whole regime will become a mess:

  - Write out the procedure and give it to the school.
  - Make sure your child knows what the procedure is and has practised the routine over and over again so it has a chance of success.
  - If the school insists that medication is the family's problem, take the issue up with education authorities, as it is a form of discrimination. If your school still insists on parental responsibility, keep the medication somewhere where it is both safe and secure and can't be forgotten — some parents wrap it in gladwrap and put it in the lunch box, some strap it to the side of a popper, one boy says that he keeps it in one of those Tic Tac containers so other kids don't know he's taking a tablet.
  - Some parents organise one of those containers that indicate daily dosage so parents and children and staff know whether the dose has been taken.
  - It's wise for both teachers and parents to highlight

the theme of individual differences — some kids are tall; some short; some fair; some dark; some need blockout outdoors (even with a sunhat), some don't; some need a puffer, some don't; some need to have injections, some don't; some need teeth braces, some don't; some wear glasses, some don't; some need to take tablets, some don't. We're all different and we're all imperfect so no one is better than anyone else, no one is more 'psycho' than anyone else, just different.

■ Above all else, whether it be glasses, tablets, braces, diet, taking blood sugar levels, putting on sunscreen or whatever, it's vital that the child be involved and preferably feel that it's their decision to go through the regime. If it's imposed by parents because it's good for their future and the kids can't see or feel the difference, then you can expect poor compliance and defiance.

DO

✓ Do talk openly with the school.

✓ Do discuss the reasons for the medication with your child and make sure you gain their full cooperation. For kids taking Ritalin, Dexamphetamine or some other ADHD medication, I say something like this: 'In our brains we have millions of brain cells which connect up to each other when we want to think or solve problems. That's why we're so smart. Some brains sometimes don't have the right amount of stuff to link the cells together so the brain goes off on the wrong track, so we forget what we've been told or we drift off and think about something else, and that can get us into big trouble. This tablet is meant to help your brain keep on track, but it only lasts for about 4 hours and that's why we sometimes need to take more at school'. I should add, that because the kids have ADHD, any longer explanation is likely to get lost; even this spiel I often accompany with drawings, or a spark plug for motor enthusiasts to show the gap and to show how it connects and fires the motor.

✓ **Do** have a good and regular routine — routine and consistency are the keys to the success of the regime.

✓ **Do** very clearly label all medication to be administered by other adults.

✓ **Do** give your kids assurance that they're one of many.

✓ **Do,** if your child is being teased, act quickly, inform the teacher (quietly) and perhaps use some teasing coping strategy — see the teasing tossing techniques suggested on page 121 — and practise a few quick one-liners; for instance, if the other kids say, 'Are you ADD?' (or any other label) your child can retort, 'Yeah, that's my problem, what's yours?'

✓ **Do** be aware that kids can fake taking their medication or throw it in the bin; that's why it's best done with adult supervision.

✓ **Do** set up a system so you know when medication is running out.

✓ **Do** make sure at home that the medication is taken at a time and place that make it difficult for the child to forget — that is, the routine is practised so often it becomes automatic, for example, taking medication before eating any breakfast or lunch.

✓ **Do** stress the difference between helpful medication from the doctor and illicit drugs.

✓ **Do** keep reviewing the arrangements with your child's doctor, as your goal should be to have your child on the minimum amounts of medication needed to function effectively.

school systems (or families), it's a time of increasing alienation from school and ultimately from society.

The middle years are a time of enormous importance and turbulence as mind, body, heart and soul all go through enormous change. Adolescence is generally thought to begin at puberty. In Australia, that's happening more and more before the kids reach high school, with girls generally reaching puberty between 9 and 14 years and boys at 10 to 15 years. Because so much change is going on at this stage, and because children are so vulnerable at times of massive change, this group needs special provision, special understanding, special curriculum and special protection.

The special features of kids at this stage include:

Physical development
- growth spurts
- wide range of differences in growth and development
- uneven growth with feet, ears and noses leading the way
- body hair and body odour become noticeable
- some gawkiness evident, as muscle coordination may lag behind muscle development

Social and emotional development
- unsure of what's appropriate behaviour at times of such rapid change, friendships can be very strained as adolescents try to play the role
- emotional highs and lows are more pronounced
- self-esteem is challenged by all the changes in their lives
- increasing sexual awareness and awareness of sexual relationships
- increasing drive to make decisions about adult roles
- increasing identification with peers whose acceptance becomes of profound importance
- increasing awareness of their own identity and values as they launch out and away from the protective umbrella of family

- increasing heights of emotions such as anxiety, love, fear, jealousy, loneliness and anger.

Intellectual development
- higher levels of abstract thinking become more apparent
- values are being formed and learned from peers
- high idealism about social and environmental, if not personal, issues
- increasing concern about life and death and mortality
- with increasing self-consciousness comes some self-centred thinking, with increasing opposition to adult edicts

During this stage of development adolescents are not children and they're not adults — they're mixed up. As one cynic said, adolescence is that stage between infancy and adultery. Today they want to assert independence by going out with friends and tonight they may behave like 8-year-olds.

Adolescents, maybe because they're trying to set themselves free of 'childish' dependency and link up with more 'mature' peer groups, risk free-falling into social oblivion as they make that voyage. It's scary — and they will search desperately for acceptance from the peer group, to gain the nod of the mob, the pat on the back from the pack. Attitudes to morality, sex, drug use, are often formed during adolescence — and much of that attitude will reflect the values of their group, their mates or their club.

So how do we help kids to thrive during this period, especially if they don't want to know what we think or what we want? As some guru said, you'll know when your family has made it through adolescence because someday, one day, the kids might just do something nice despite the fact that you asked them to do it.

Transition to middle or high school

Every parent thinks about the trauma associated with beginning primary school. We often forget that there are just as many and often just as scary transitions to high or middle school. Although all kids hate the fall from top dog at primary school to underdog at high school, toughing it out is all part of adolescent initiation rites. The symptoms of stress may be the same as for younger kids (tears, tummy-aches, tiredness, testiness) but they're much less open about how they feel so your help must be much less open too.

If you have a choice in which school they will attend here are some steps to take:

1. During the first half of their final year in primary school:
   - Talk to parents of high/middle school aged children and gain their impressions of local schools, how much they involve parents, how much they listen to parents, and ask a few questions about the school's priorities. Here are a few things you could include on your school shopping list when talking to other parents or teachers at the potential schools or glean from the school's annual report:
     - academic performance of school
     - curriculum
     - student welfare policy
     - discipline code
     - incentive system
     - class structures
     - school and student leadership
     - learning support
     - role of sport/music/performing arts, etc.
   - Talk to friends who are teachers at local middle/high schools about their perceptions, school culture, school strengths and transition support from primary school.
   - Talk to primary teachers about your child's special needs (if any), their strengths, weaknesses, other kids who might be going to your preferred high/middle school, key contact people at the new middle/high school and about timelines for specialist school entry (e.g. selective schools, performing arts schools).
   - Talk to your child about their preferences, their peer

group movements, their interests and strengths, their
concerns and fears.

- Approach high/middle schools about their curriculum,
  welfare code, etc. (as outlined above), meet key staff
  and ask for a tour to see what the 'working school'
  looks and feels like. Get their timelines for enrolment.

2. When the school to be attended is decided:
   - Accept or appeal depending on the decision.
   - Enquire about their orientation programs and any
     student information booklets outlining policies,
     uniform, etc.
   - If your child has special learning needs, medication
     needs or illness management needs, make sure these are
     clarified with the school and specifically with the
     upcoming year coordinator or equivalent.
   - Clarify the procedures for day one at the new school —
     bus routes or travel arrangements, dress requirements,
     uniform for specialist subjects, procedures for lateness
     or absence, location of student welfare staff, timetable
     diary, hours of attendance, etc.

3. In the first term at the new school:
   - Talk to your kids about their experiences and
     adjustments.
   - Contact the student adviser or other welfare staff if you
     have any concerns (bullying, academic progress, peer
     conflict, etc.).
   - Try to join in parent volunteer groups (canteen, P & F,
     P & C, Learning Centre, mentor mum program, etc.).
   - Encourage the kids to 'join in' the new school as kids
     tend to get out of a school what they put in. Encourage
     their involvement in sports, debating, clubs, bands,
     computer group, animal nursery — whatever suits their
     interests and the school has to offer.
   - If you have financial concerns that might affect or
     prevent your child's involvement in certain clubs or
     electives or excursions, make sure the school knows —

sometimes there are special 'discretionary' funds that schools can tap for some activities.

- As a general rule you'll be doing the right thing if you follow these suggestions.

DO

✓ **Do** attend any orientation nights and become familiar with routines, expectations, responsibilities at first-hand rather than by rumour.

✓ **Do** make sure the kids know the route, the layout and preferably a few kids to hang about with until they get their feet.

✓ **Do** be involved in the school in some way such as canteen, parent committee, working bees or whatever so the kids know their education is important to you and you know what's going on around the place.

✓ **Do** expect a bit of an attempt to copy older high school kids, just as young kids copied them at primary; it's their way of gaining acceptance, feeling grown up and adjusting to their new identity.

✓ **Do** be practical and reasonable so that what you ask doesn't put them at obvious odds with their mates or isolate them; those scars they can wear for years and you'll pay the bills.

✓ **Do** keep the communication lines well and truly greased during the transition to middle/high school; if kids can just talk things through with parents then they'll be able to cope with the incredible changes that high school demands. That means having real time to just be with your kids, it can't simply be packaged into some marketing mumbo-jumbo called 'quality time'.

✓ **Do** help set up good home routines so homework has a place and time and priority.

✓ **Do** make sure they keep up with sports or hobbies or

other interests that help to salvage an ailing ego, particularly if they're not brilliant students.

✓ **Do** try to be positive. For any child of any age, feelings about school will be drastically affected by parental attitudes; if you're nervous, they're nervous, if you don't like the teacher then chances are nor will they. There's nothing more damaging to kids' morale than a divorce between home and school.

DON'T

✗ **Don't** over-react to all the rumours about heads being dunked down the toilet and other horrific welcomes; they're no more than legends and I've yet to meet the child who has actually had it happen or can even name a victim.

✗ **Don't** overprotect them by fussing over forgotten lunches, bus passes, or even fall outs with friends; at early adolescence their brains are nearing their peak and they're well and truly able to creatively work their way out of trouble.

✗ **Don't** overintrude too early just because they're having a few settling-in worries; too much parent protection can deprive them of a lifetime of self-confidence.

✗ **Don't** overdo your response to new friends; by early adolescence friendships are very important and the kids need to feel them out at their own pace without parental pacemakers.

✗ **Don't** overdo the individuality ethos; they don't like to be different at that age so be sensitive to their need to belong and be the same as their mates.

CASE STUDY

Andrew

School had been a breeze for Andrew, a smart but sensitive 11-year-old, until he got to high school. A Year 9 bully decided that Andrew was fair game and hounded him day and night. Andrew began to feel terrified not only of going to school but even of leaving the house. So this young computer whiz spent his days curled up on his bed or locked in his room. When his perplexed parents threatened to force him back to school he tried to make an attempt (albeit a clumsy one) on his own life.

His level of panic made progress hard work. His parents believed that a naturopathic anxiety-fighting formula helped, and we removed the blame and shame component of their management. Once it started to settle down we grabbed on to his interest in electronics and computers. We drew up a fear-flow diagram with a series of binary (yes–no) choices, beginning with the easiest level and

working towards his panic level. The first question was
simply, 'Are you afraid all the time?' Andrew confidently
chose 'No' to that question, so we moved to the next level
and then to the next until he was forced to answer 'Yes'.
In that way he was able to see how far he had progressed
and we were able to work out tactics to topple his next
panic point — and so on. The school was great and the
home — school liaison officer put enormous time into
visiting and preparing him for his return; bully was barred
from any contact and put on a good behaviour contract.

Yesterday Andrew phoned to tell me he'd not only made
it to school but he'd actually spent the last two days in
the classroom and he felt very pleased. A big incentive for
Andrew was that his parents offered $1 towards some
electronics equipment every day he achieved a new goal.

Early adolescent needs — home and school

Regardless of whether the kids are early or late maturers, big
or little, every adolescent feels a loss of confidence because of
the enormous physical, social and sexual changes, and very few
escape the dreaded acne. Nothing preoccupies their minds or
their hands or their mirrors more than the zit! You can't fast-
forward this stage but there are several ways home can help.
Here are a few important ways:

- Emphasise the good things they do, not the bad.
- Take their ideas and feelings seriously.
- Define limits and rules very clearly and enforce them —
  but do allow for growth and change as they mature.
  From the time the kids take their first step they're
  growing up and away, we can't stop it, we can't over-
  hurry it, we just have to keep balancing their freedoms
  with the responsibilities they show they're ready for.
- Be a good role model.
- Teach them how to budget money and time.
- Set goals with them that can be reached.

- Give them responsibility!!
- Spend time together and be available for them.
- Talk with them about their interests and sport — try and attend some events with them.
- Discuss problems with them but don't keep blaming failures in their character (too selfish, too pig-headed, etc.); keep to the problem, not the personality.
- Show them you love them, hug them, tell them you love them; at times they may be less than forthcoming in reply but that's understandable.
- Read their vibes on how and when they like to receive parental hugs and kisses.
- Treat them the way you'd like to be treated.
- Involve them in rule-setting decisions.
- Help them accept the consequences of their decisions.
- Encourage them to be involved in their community, in sport or fundraising or in causes that appeal to their values.

But remember — no matter what you might think the young adolescent might think about their family, research consistently shows that family is the number one source of emotional support and number one concern. For instance, in a statistical review of calls to Kids Help Line, family relationships were by far the single biggest issue, for both boys and girls. In a 1999 study done by Dangar Research, again for Kids Help Line, this age group (more accurately 8–15-year-olds) put parents way out in front as top role models, with other relatives second and sport stars third. However, problems often arise when the adults in their lives don't live up to the very high ideals this group puts on all its values — it's not surprising that the same survey found that many adolescents thought that adults behaved hypocritically.

Educational needs of the young adolescent

Various State education authorities and the Australian Curriculum Studies Association have come out strongly in suggesting the urgency of special schooling provisions, curriculum and staffing for the young adolescent in the middle years. The suggestions include the following:

- Smaller class or learning group sizes to help students feel free to share, talk and ask, and to maximise the opportunities for students to be involved in their own education so they do not become alienated.
- Smaller group or school size so that the individual doesn't become swamped by the 'mob'; the whole idea for these kids is to feel part of a 'team'. If the school is large then maybe sub-schools or teams could be formed.
- Team teaching, so the student is being treated as a whole person, rather than subject-specific teaching; this would use students' time and space more effectively than nomading their way around the school to the next subject specialist.
- Curriculum that takes notice of their need to work through their feelings and values.
- Involvement of parents so that the education is really a team effort.
- Genuine consultation between staff and students about their views.
- Student participation in decision-making.
- Varied approaches to education that involved more discussion, small group work and interactive learning, and less of the talk-and-chalk style that students found boring and alienating.
- Practical learning where students were encouraged to learn from hands-on experience.
- High emphasis on pastoral care: by reducing the number of teachers involved with a student it is possible to develop higher levels of trust and rapport and more involvement in learning. Some systems use a single teacher as home-teacher to take a supportive role with their charge and to ensure that the student is treated as a whole person.

Tips from teachers

✍ Teachers suggested that every class dealing with young adolescents highlight the importance of individual differences and the nature of education as a collaborative process between teacher and pupil.

✍ 'For older girls, even before they become self-conscious about slow maturing, flat chests, etc. I talk in class about different models and heroes from TV, the small, the different, the Ally McBeals of the world, so the pumped up *Baywatch* image is put in its place.'

Sexual development and body image

Early maturers

You probably know that today's children are taller and heavier and that they mature sexually earlier than ever before in history. It is common for girls to reach puberty in their primary school years. This transformation may be normal, natural and healthy, but for kids who feel different to their peers, it poses problems. For a boy, having a beard in Year 7 may be a huge status symbol. But early maturation for a fifth-grade girl can trigger a real crisis in self-confidence; she feels different and self-conscious and often becomes very sensitive.

If you have an early maturing daughter who has become secretive or self-conscious, then the local doctor may be able to reassure you that she is handling her periods sensibly and safely.

One way to get such reassurance is perhaps to arrange an appointment for your daughter on some pretext or other, having a quiet word with the doctor beforehand about your concerns and letting his or her years of tactful experience do the rest. It's not hard for a doctor to raise questions innocently about your daughter's level of awareness of the changes that happen to girls around her age, what she should do if her periods start, how to be prepared, how to handle an emergency at school, and so on. Given that 75 per cent of teachers are female, there's every chance that there's a woman on the primary school staff whom the girls are able to relate to easily on these issues. If it hasn't already been done, it might be timely for you to ask that teacher to call the senior girls together and explain the school procedures and facilities in case they are ever needed.

Unfortunately many primary school uniforms, such as sports T-shirts, are not designed with pubescent girls in mind, and can cause anything from embarrassment to ridicule to sports aversion, or even school aversion, if the situation is not sensitively handled. It's a good idea to ask at the school office or even at a local department store for suggestions about undervests or training bras.

As research shows that girls tend to experience more self-consciousness than boys regarding early maturity, here are some do's and don'ts for early maturing girls.

DO

✓ Do caution your child against telling the world or boasting about having her periods; kids often don't realise the complications that can be caused by loose tongues.

✓ Do check if and where the school has a special girls' room, and what supplies it stocks; perhaps you could make a donation to ensure that adequate supplies are kept there.

✓ Do keep a calendar record as a reminder in the initial stages, although there is no need to worry if early periods are irregular.

✓ Do give a little extra comfort and reassurance generally — this is a time of insecurity for most girls.

✓ Do talk in positive terms about growing up and maturing.

✓ Do look for appropriate and discreet clothing.

✓ Do make sure your child is well informed about upcoming bodily changes so that confusion isn't added to consternation.

DON'T

✗ **Don't** put sanitary items in her bag 'just in case' — nosey boys may tease her. Perhaps they could be placed discreetly in a side pocket of a multi-zip school bag.

✗ **Don't** tease or make jokes; it may be funny to us, but it's terribly personal for the kids.

✗ **Don't** fuss about it all. I find today's kids remarkably competent and independent in the self-management of their periods. The availability of easy-to-use products has made this stage much easier for today's young women.

✗ **Don't** treat it as a problem; it's progress.

✗ **Don't** start tying adult insecurities and anxieties to her development (e.g. telling her that now she must be careful, behave like an adult, etc.) or the changes taking place will carry considerable fear and self-consciousness.

Late maturers

In some ways there are just as many problems for girls as there are for boys if they are late maturers. The boys get called 'shorty', 'shrimp', 'pint-size', 'Tom Thumb', 'squirt', and other less flattering and less printable names, which can give some small kids the proverbial 'little man' complex that is very hard to shake. For the girls who are left standing flat-chested at the school gate while their friends put on make-up that makes them look twice their age, late maturation can be soul-destroying.

With both groups those who can feel it most are their families, as the kids grapple with feelings of inferiority as their friends leave them behind. Expect a bit of over-reaction and compensation as these children try to make up the difference. Good friends, a good home and the patience of Job will see you through, but if your child is dropping behind their growth norms for no apparent reason, then talk to your doctor about it. Overall, parents are probably never more important than at this time.

Body image
Perhaps the biggest issue facing the young adolescent, every day, in every way, in every mirror, is the issue of body image at a time of so much change. Body image becomes a preoccupation for many teenagers. The zit is not just a pimple, it's a blight on their image, and they hate it. It's so hard for adolescents to feel stable and secure at a time when everything is changing so fast. Research among adolescents has found that most dislike some aspect of their appearance — nose too long, chest too flat, eyes too far apart, ears too flappy, hips too big, etc. Girls particularly can go to enormous lengths to change their body shape or hide the shame of their shape. It's not surprising to find the increasingly image-conscious adolescent girl at the forefront of rises in teenage smoking and eating disorders, or obsessively over-exercising, or taking laxatives, or wearing baggy clothes, or hiding out at home, or sulking, or vomiting up their food. Boys are perhaps somewhat less prone to image obsession but will hide their self-consciousness behind brazen drug-taking, risk-taking, steroid-use or excessive exercise/gym work.

How to help?
- One way is to have a good book or two around. There are so many now it would be silly to try and list them but I really like the more recent book by Bronwyn Donaghy, *Unzipped* — it's so practical and starts from where kids really are. I also like the Impact book *No is Not Enough: Helping Teenagers Avoid Assault*. There are also some excellent books recommended by the Family Planning Association, including Darvill and Powell's books *The Puberty Book* and *What Shall We Tell the Children?*.
- Another way is to talk — but adolescents aren't always the easiest people to talk to, so choose times and tactics that suit timetables and personalities. Often driving together in the car is a good time to talk where closeness yet absence of eye-contact drops the defences. Sometimes

it's best by their bedside or walking the dog in the dark where the night brings its own closeness. But certainly the biggest dangers leading to premature sex are ignorance and loneliness. In his book *Growing Pains* David Bennett sums up the research this way: 'More adolescent virgins than nonvirgins feel closer to, better understood by and have easier communication with their parents who are more likely to have discussed sexual matters with them.' Again it comes home to us, that in this day and age of so much materialism, our kids would be so much better off if we spent half as much money on them and twice as much time.

Teacher comment

✍ Dear Dr John — I'm a male English teacher and am responding to your invitation for comment and advice to parents for your new book. Let me share one of the less seamy sections of a story in a girl's notebook she handed to me after class recently.

'He silently carried me to bed and gently lay me down. I really loved this man, We stripped and then he climbed onto the bed and straddled himself on top of me. I reached up to him and ran my fingers through his thick curly hair and he bent down to nuzzle my breasts and play with them. The sparks of electricity that ran through my body were indescribable, My skin was flushed and my body arched towards him.

You can imagine the rest. She's just 13 years old, she told me she has been sexually abused by Mum's boyfriend and the boyfriend's sons (when their dad was busy with Mum) since she was 8. She doesn't feel angry about it, in fact elsewhere in the notebook she says how much she treasured their touch. It's all pretty sad but she also writes that it's not sex she's after, just someone to hold her and cuddle her, which, she says, her busy mum never does, and she has no dad.

The case has since been reported to authorities and she has been getting counselling now (hopefully Mum is too), but my reasons for writing are not only to alert your readers to the predicaments many teachers face every day in high schools but, through your book, hopefully shake up some parents who are either so slack they don't care or so preoccupied they're not really offering any parental protection. Yet if we dare tell parents, often they either blame us or ground their kids, but never take the blame or change their own behaviour. Parents MUST listen and share and cuddle their kids or they'll go out and hire a hug. It makes me mad to see nice kids going down the tube so I'm letting off steam in the hope it helps some kid somewhere.
Glen

Eating disorders

Everything seems to be happening for kids at an earlier age than a generation ago, including eating disorders. We now have a rapidly increasing rate of obesity among the young and cases of bulimia and anorexia in children as young as 8! Certainly as their bodies change, young people become increasingly sensitive about their body shape. The modern more sedentary lifestyle often produces overweight children, but on the other hand shape-sensitive young people, particularly girls, will often attempt to alter nature in ways their body was never meant to go, and sometimes that produces a dangerous mindset which can be hard to shift.

Overeating

According to a Harvard University study there has been a 39 per cent increase in obesity in young people and a 64 per cent increase in super-obesity over the past 25 years. That might be great for the annual tug-o-war fight but not for the fight for life; nearly half the overweight children go on to have weighty problems later on, including high blood pressure, heart attack, stroke, diabetes, chest and lung problems, cancer, etc.

Apparently our TV advertising is not helping the problem. According to Rosemary Stanton, leading Australian dietitian, children who watched TV between 3.30 p.m. and 6 p.m. over the five weeknights were urged to eat foods with a total of 700 grams of salt, 8 kilograms of fat and 19 kilograms of sugar. Yet we all know that being fat is not only a health hazard — with diet being responsible in some way for 60 per cent of deaths — but that fat kids are also teased and have very low self-esteem. As well, a recent British study has shown that kids with a poor diet do not perform as well at school or in IQ tests.

For whatever reason, an overweight adolescent is usually an unhappy adolescent, so what should parents do?

DO

✓ Do have only healthy snack foods around the house. This means the kids can graze happily and it takes the weight off your mind and their bodies at the same time. The message is to make food good, not god!

✓ Do encourage good eating habits, too, and don't be too shy about joining the call for more greening and graining of school canteens.

✓ Do limit the time they spend in front of TV (substitute 'computer', 'Internet' or 'video games') as research is clear that the avid viewers generally are less healthy and carry more weight than their more active peers. Get them outside in games, sport, delivering messages, and if possible let them walk or ride to school ... and if they complain, well, even that's using up energy.

✓ Do make sure kids feel your love. It's worth remembering that for many overeaters it's a psychological hunger which no diet will ever satisfy. Many may be eating away their anger, chewing on stress, swallowing their pride or just starving for love ... and food can give a safe quick fix.

✓ Do lead by example!

DON'T

✗ **Don't** focus on the fat. Stress seems to stimulate the sweet tooth. Ask the child's doctor to talk to them about easy diets. Remember that the goal is to make them feel spick without too much span.

✗ **Don't** use food as a bribe.

✗ **Don't** keep junk food in the house. If there is no unhealthy food around, and if the *whole family* sticks to sensible eating habits and a healthy lifestyle, it can't fail to help. Kids may not listen very well, but they never fail to copy.

✗ **Don't** believe that 'chubby' means 'healthy'; early fat cells are awfully hard to lose.

✗ **Don't** put lots of sweets in with your children's lunches.

✗ **Don't** give them too much pocket money to waste.

Overeating problem?
Check for the following tendencies:
• gulps food down with excess gusto and greed
• is considered by the doctor to be overweight
• sneaks or steals food from home or other lunches
• craves food, especially junk food
• eats a lot of junk, but then can't eat a proper meal
• has parents with an overeating problem

Seek professional advice if:
• your child has an addiction to sweets or chocolates
• your child is drinking constantly
• your child's appetite changes suddenly
• your child steals food
• certain foods seem to make your child edgy and irritable

CASE STUDY

Damien

Damien was a big lump of a kid, who hated his school nickname ('Dinosaur') even if it fitted him better than his clothes. Damien was a gentle giant with an old-fashioned mum who really believed that a healthy boy had a bit of beef on him. Over time, eating had become his dominant passion, especially after his dad left home. It became his dominant pastime, too, because he had no friends. So he started to skip school, to stay at home and eat even more.

We talked to Damien about things he would like to do to have fun, and then worked out that these things would be easier if he felt fitter. Dad agreed to take him horse-riding on his access weekends if Damien rode over on his bike (and even that took some training). His mum agreed that the whole family had to shape up a bit, so she changed her shopping priorities, joined Weight Watchers and took Damien along to a paediatric dietitian. So far, so good for Damien; he has never been healthier or happier.

Undereating — food rejection

Most pubescent and adolescent girls, and increasingly more boys, become weight conscious and, reinforced by the slim magazine message, join the race of wishful shrinkers. For most it's all just part of adjustment to growing up, for others it becomes a lifelong preoccupation and for a few (2–4 per cent) it can develop into a real problem, manifested as bulimia or anorexia nervosa. Some of the early signs that they're developing unhealthy attitudes include the following:

- becoming cranky if people talk about diet
- storing food in bedroom
- becoming sick after eating
- never really enjoying eating
- believing that they're fat, although looks and scales say otherwise.

159

It becomes a problem requiring professional intervention if it involves:

- continual rejection of food
- refusal to maintain body weight
- more than 25 per cent loss of what would have been their weight
- intense fear of becoming obese — almost as if they become psychologically allergic to any body fat at all
- recurrent episodes of binge eating
- binge consumption of high calorie food
- self-induced vomiting
- reliance on diet tablets or laxatives to help control weight
- belief that they have no control over their eating behaviour.
- chronic constipation
- exercising to exhaustion
- cessation of periods.

We're not sure of the causes. Obviously our society's odd obsession with fattening food and slim figures doesn't help. But there's also a mixture of biology, personal crisis and home hassling involved. So what can we do if we're worried?

DO

✓ Do keep healthy food in the house. The best idea for preventing anorexia or bulimia is to have healthy food around and not worry so much what they do or don't eat.

✓ Do visit the doctor. Use some other pretext (e.g. an iron level check or problems with their periods), not food, to trigger a visit to the doctor — maybe phone ahead so the doctor is well briefed and can steer them to expert medical and psychological help.

DON'T

✗ Don't expect young people, even if they're dizzy or

struggling, to admit they are anorexic. Some see that as a small price to pay to keep the dreaded weight at bay.

✗ **Don't** nag about food or weight, as the problem might stem from nagging or over-control in the first place.

✗ **Don't** ignore it. With medical help and family therapy the problem can often be overcome but it's a serious problem and one that should be tackled *professionally* if you have any concerns.

CASE STUDY
Dianna

Dianna was just 14 and an only child. She was bright, vivacious, strongly principled and very much her father's daughter. She believed strongly in honesty, hated hypocrisy and really went to bat for the underdog. As she faced the adolescent agonies over drugs, sex, alcohol, smoking, truanting and partying, she repelled them easily at first, knowing she was right and the peers were wrong. As she grew older, these torments didn't subside and she felt a growing urge to experiment, to break out and to answer the 'daddy's girl' taunts.

It wasn't long before her conflict found its form in food. Dianna would be given a nutritious lunch by her mother but felt tempted by junk food. Having tasted of the forbidden fruit and to prevent being punished, Dianna would then go home and regurgitate the lot, as her form of purging herself of all the evil. Dianna was showing clear signs of bulimia.

The good news for Dianna is that because she admitted that she had a problem and was early in calling for help the prognosis is reasonably positive. As should be the case for any bulimic or anorexic problem, Dianna was immediately put into contact with the specialist Eating Disorder Unit at the regional hospital and is in a long-term outpatient program. Like any good therapy program it involves a combination of strategies: medication, dietary management, cognitive behavioural therapy to address her thought distortions, and some highly promising family therapy.

Anorexia nervosa sufferers more often have to undertake an intense long-term inpatient program and their prognosis is much more cautious.

Motivation — especially of boys

I've included this new section in this chapter because the motivation of boys appears to be an issue endemic (at least in our culture), not to young kids but to the maturing boy. Recently I met with the Heads of Welfare in all the schools in our area — public and private. When I asked them to name the issue inside their classrooms that they were most concerned about, they were unanimous in nominating the motivation of boys as the critical issue — boys who were glassy-eyed at school, boys who couldn't care less about academic merit, boys who wouldn't even go up and receive a school award because it wasn't cool, boys who didn't try any more. This is not an isolated problem; the decline in HSC performance by boys is worrying testimony to the fact that schools are struggling to motivate their males.

Many schools are addressing this problem through involving the boys in developing school rules, welfare policies, freedoms and responsibilities, privileges and penalties. Although boys respect and respond to power, they also tend to copy it! Some schools use natural or logical consequences, which kids understand and respect much more than nagging or overprotecting. Some operate on various forms of 'levels' of behaviour. For instance, students, parents and teachers may work out which behaviours (good and bad) should be assigned to which level, and how many repeats of the behaviour deserve a shift (up or down) of level. At each positive level certain privileges might apply, such as first choice of sport, special canteen line, special library borrowing rights, special excursions, etc. If children slipped down into the negative levels privileges would be lost and, if the kids slipped further, parents would be called up and penalties would apply (such as last choice of sport, no excursions, detentions, suspension, exclusion, etc.). The advantage of this system is that the boys have helped design the code and it's very hard for anyone to disobey their own rules.

But the research is clear (see Steve Biddulph's book *Raising Boys*) that much has to be done at home if boys are to regain their belief in themselves. And the research is also clear that the key home figure in boys' self-esteem (and therefore their motivation) is Dad! In an age when only 1 in 4 teachers is male, and where more and more dads are disappearing off the domestic front, this is indeed a tragedy and a social crisis. In the days gone by dads worked just as hard, probably spending nearly as much time away from home as they do now, but there was the 'tribe' to back up the home — uncles, neighbours and grandfathers were more easily and readily available to give boys the role models and firm love they needed. Now it's all up to the nuclear family to deliver the lot — and it's not happening. According to 1999 ABS figures, the average adult male works 47 hours — that's the equivalent of a 6-day week — and over one-third work more than 53 hours. Add to that the increasing amount of time commuting to work as housing moves further and further out of town, and it's not surprising that many dads are missing in action, presumed preoccupied.

Fathers who try to do their job as fathers the same way their dad did will find it won't work as well, because 62 per cent of mums are at work and not at home to pick up the pieces, and because the extended male family is not there to fill in the gaps. The stereotypic work ethic, with minimal display of affection and relying on the use of aggression to resolve problems, is no use to a boy growing up in today's world. Mothers who consistently use a soft role also don't help.

My colleague Peter Clarke, who works in our clinic with angry and unmotivated adolescent males, uses William Glasser's control theory as the basis of his therapy. It hinges on five basic needs — the basic need for survival and then the four psychological needs of belonging, power, freedom and fun. Boys need to have all four psychological needs met to be motivated to change the way they do things. Examples of each are:

Belonging
- time spent alone with Dad, Mum and friends
- team sport, clubs or groups (e.g. Scouts, Air Cadets)
- peer outings (excursions, mates over, trips)

Power
- cooking for self (and cleaning up!)
- doing jobs around the house — taking responsibility for some part of domestic life (e.g. pool, pets, room, lawn, garbage, computer roster, etc.)
- receiving and managing pocket money

Freedom (provided the choice does not impact unfairly on others or impede their freedom)
- choices in outings, mates, party invitees
- selection of books to be borrowed from library
- timing for doing daily routines and jobs
- self-care of body hygiene

Fun
- playing on the computer
- some form of indoor and outdoor entertainment
- physical activity with others
- roughhouse play, jokes and humour-sharing with parents

Although dads' weekday times may be limited by work or access restrictions, much can be made up over the weekend if dads are willing and can put aside work worries so their kids feel that they matter. Depending on family style, that weekend time could include sharing in their sport, helping them with jobs (or vice versa), helping them get a meal or two ready, helping them tidy their room, playing on the computer together, watching TV or a movie together, helping them build or make things, sharing stories (e.g. about what we like, don't like, biggest mistakes, biggest fear, favourite hero/team, etc.). The earlier the bond between father and son is cemented the better; as boys grow older it's normal for them to challenge or dismiss 'the old man' as off the pace. I think it was Mark Twain who said at the age of 16 that he couldn't believe how dumb his dad was but how much he had learned by the time he turned 21!

CASE STUDY
Billy

'This Ritalin medication's not working', says Billy's desperate mum. 'He's still impossible to get out of bed in the morning, still can't get him off his Game Boy or computer, still being really nasty to other kids at school and although I hate myself doing it, I find I end up smacking him again and again just to do as he's told. Why won't he? He's got everything — TV, video and computer in his room, gets everything he wants, meals he wants, meals in his room if he wants. His father and I would do anything for him but nothing seems to make him any happier or easier to handle.'

Yes, Dad had supplied everything to meet his every want but this kid was suffering from neglect! No one was meeting his *needs!* Where was Dad? Working late nights and overseas to give him everything, except what he needed: firm love, leadership, rules, encouragement, fun, fantasy, family who enjoy being and sharing. Mum's nurturing love was no match for this active, electronically obsessive boy.

Only when I told the parents that 'Dilly Billy' (the name kids gave him at school) was suffering from neglect did I get his horrified father taking stock. We can't buy our kids happiness, the best thing fathers can give their kids is their time.

Strategies

Here are some suggestions to improve the adolescent boy's motivation:

- Self-motivation must be the goal for any growing boy.
- Finding their niche or areas of talent so they feel they belong, can have fun and are worthwhile humans.
- Helping them take responsibility for their own action.
- Structured positive activity shared with family, hopefully including Dad.
- Listening to them so they feel that it's not 'woosy' to share or to express fears.
- 1:1 time spent with each parent.
- Boys respond to encouragement and tangible rewards so use pocket money or domestic part-time work payment as a way of gaining cooperation and independence (for jobs done, not for just being there).
- Boys respond to challenge, especially physical. Where possible their style of education must take into account their need to be physical, to contest, to risk-take, to pit themselves against opposition (e.g. time, peers, logical problem, physical challenge) and against the elements (e.g. nature, wilderness).
- Boys respond well in these middle years to male role models — and as there are fewer at home, the more the need for good adult role models among teachers.

Schools can't rely only on the awards and certificates that may have been used in primary school. As young adolescents are so sensitive about not being little kids any more, they will reject those strategies that were used on them when they were younger. Incentives relevant to their maturity should be used— movie passes, first choice of sport, access to the gym or basketball court, etc.

Depression and suicide

It's a sad commentary on today's world that a section on suicide and depression needs to be included in any book regarding children. But because the rate of suicide has jumped by 450 per cent over the past 20 years and because it's every parent's worst fear, it has to be addressed in this revised edition. The sad facts are that even just from 1996 to 1997 (last figures available), there was an increase of 22 per cent, with attempts by young males up 25 per cent and by females up 19 per cent (Australian Bureau of Statistics), with 510 young people between the ages of 15 and 24 committing suicide (417 males and 93 females). But there is some better news for parents of children aged 4 to 13 years:

- The incidence of completed suicides is very, very rare in this age group, with fewer than 12 suicide deaths annually, nationally.
- Every child in this age group faces problems that seem too complex to handle; many, many, maybe most, will at some stage say they wish they were dead, life's not worth living, why were they ever born, they're going to kill themselves — it doesn't mean they'll do it. It does mean that it's a cry for help. Such statements are almost inevitable given the pace and pressure of modern life, the breakdown of the ties that bind them to the planet and the attention death attracts in the media.
- Every child must experience sadness or there'd be no such thing as happiness. This doesn't mean they're suffering from debilitating, demotivating, destabilising depression. However, in some busy and preocccupied families, acting down rather than acting up may be a better way of winning attention without attracting punishment. Research is also clear that children who lack 'resilience' are more prone to depression and to be 'at risk'.
- Depressed or chronically sad children will not perform well in the classroom as they are too preoccupied with their own problems and lack the mental energy necessary to participate effectively in the classroom (or playground).
- Depression may take different forms, with twice as many girls diagnosed with depression as males. More

males than females talk down but act out their depression with bullying, risk taking, aggression, defiance, rebellion and non-cooperation. More females than males talk up but act down their depression with features such as sustained sadness, loss of fun, loss of energy, loss of interest in relationships, and feeling sick.

Depression checklist

- feels worthless
- seems and looks sad
- talks about self-harm
- sulks a lot
- cries a lot
- needs to be perfect
- tries to hurt themself
- anxious about everything
- feels no-one loves them
- feels everyone picks on them
- feels a sense of hopelessness or helplessness
- feelings of boredom
- depressed emotions or body language
- preoccupation with death
- feels guilty about everything
- very self-conscious
- worries that they might do something bad
- lonely and feels they have no friends
- very nervous
- self-mutilates

If your child is showing strong symptoms of more than 6 of these characteristics, then chances are that they are depressed and in need of help.

Here's what you can do to help

1. Perception check-up — check them out through the eyes of the teacher or others who know them well and know how they behave away from home (e.g.

grandparent). If the symptoms shrink away from home then a good 'shrink' to look at what's going on at home may be all that's needed.

2. Medical check-up — if others agree that your child is sad get them fully checked out medically as there could be a number of things depressing their systems — anaemia, thyroid, glandular fever, allergies or food intolerances ... anything which makes them feel off the pace or not coping.

3. Situational check-up—
   - if it's all the time then a psychological check-up is needed
   - if it's just after exertion (exercise, game, sport, playgroup, full day at preschool, etc.) then a medical check is needed
   - if it's after school then an educational check is needed
   - if it's just at home then a marital and parent depression check is needed
   - if it's just before meals then it may be blood sugars are down and the answer may be having healthy snack food easily available
   - if it's just when brothers and sisters are around then it's quaintly called 'sibling rivalry'.

4. Home tone check-up — from my clinical experience the more common depressors appear to be divorce, family friction, exposure to stressful life events, parental depression, new baby, favouritism, parents too busy, or 'special' (e.g. disabled, chronically ill) brother or sister.

DO

✓ **Do** spend time with each child each day so they can offload their problems before they become depressing.

✓ **Do** make sure everyone in the family knows that you love them; tell them often and show it often — in action, not just in gifts, or they'll be more interested in money than Mummy.

✓ **Do** encourage exercise. It has been shown to be a major counter to depression — if your kids are involved in regular and enjoyable physical activity, that will engender the endorphins in the brain to help shift the depressive cloud.

✓ **Do** encourage them to link up with other like-minded people. Social glue is what bonds each of us to this earth — if your kids can find their niche in groups or activities that link them up with others, then they're hooked into life — it often shifts their self-image from ugly duckling to beautiful swan that had been swimming all alone or in the wrong pool.

✓ **Do** stop the nosedive. Some kids catastrophise — some little set-back sees the nosedive into depression (nothing works, they're no good at anything, they knew this would happen because only bad things happen to them). Help them to think about an image or action that intervenes and stops the catastrophic nosedive. If they say that they can't, then try to challenge them with this thought — 'Just as your mind is so clever that it can create the problem, so, too, if we work hard enough on it we can make up the image to beat it'. Some kids enjoy that challenge, but if they don't then it may be they need to talk about what they will do. Again it is their problem and it's only by their success that they get the lift out of the depression.

✓ **Do** have a good hard look at how the family is working on the child's resilience. *Studies have found that it's not the pressure on the individual that is the overload but the person's resilience under pressure!* Resilient kids tend to be optimistic — they don't just live the problem but actively try to solve it; they are alert and not overly dependent on others. This critical factor for survival comes from many directions. Kids tend to be more resilient if they live in hopeful, helpful and connected communities. Kids tend to be resilient if their families are hopeful and optimistic and have taught their kids some of the following: how to resolve problems; how to manage conflict; how to relate warmly; how to deal with criticism; how to assert; how to worry productively; how to offload stress; how to communicate effectively.

For other ideas on handling sadness and depression read my recent book *Who'd Be a Parent?: The Manual That Should Have Come With the Kids*.

CASE STUDY
Untying the knot

> Peter's parents broke up. Mum got custody and got depressed, Dad got mad and got out, and Peter, as you could guess, got both mad and depressed and got the tummy-aches that wore his inner pain. Later on Dad and his new partner asked to have Peter for the holidays. Many solicitor bills later it happened; it worked well and Peter asked Mum if he could stay. Mum threatened to get rid of his dog, Sally, if he didn't come back. So back came the tummies, tears and even suicide threats.
>
> Fortunately his step-mum stepped in. She got a stay of execution on the grounds of intestinal insanity and got a few things started with him including sport and unloading worry time every bed time.
>
> Peter was feeling better but the sad part is I had another call the other day, not from Peter but from Welfare, to say that Peter's gone back home to his mum and the tummy-aches have come back.
>
> When will some parents learn that no matter how much they've been hurt, unless they handle divorce sensibly they don't really untie the knot, they just shift it!

Suicidal signals

Approximately 1 in 4 school children think about suicide some time and, according to Dr James Harrison from the

National Injury Surveillance Unit, about 96 young people attempt suicide per week. This is an alarming statistic. Over 90 per cent of suicides have relayed warning signs that may have gone unaddressed. The danger signs of a child being at risk include detailed planning of the method of suicide, alcohol or drug abuse, repeated threats to suicide, previous attempts, emotional problems or the recent death of one of their close friends or a family member. Other potential indicators include many accidents, morbid themes in writing, drawing or viewing, dangerous risk-taking behaviour, and giving away favourite possessions.

When you see worrying signs ask your child what is happening — confront them directly as to whether they have thought about suicide. That gets the issue out in the open and then together you can see a way forward. If they don't or won't take any action then consult a psychologist or family doctor yourself or read one of the following:

- *Be a Friend for Life: Preventing Youth Suicide* by M. Appleby
- *Leaving Early* by Bronwyn Donaghy.

Teacher comment

✍ 'I think a lot of depression comes from parents expecting kids to be perfect, maybe because they haven't got the time to fix things if they're not. We weren't perfect, so why should they be? I think our job is to find something special to love even if the child is difficult, and surely that's not too hard.'

The work ethic — the critical component in education

Parents talk about trying to get their kids to study, to take work seriously, to perform well in exams — but none of this will be a problem if in the early and middle years of schooling the kids develop a really good work ethic. That's what brings success and that's what brings employment, not marks! The work ethic is simply an attitude towards work that enables good work to be done — its features obviously include trying hard, doing a good job, showing good application, willingness to learn, willingness to accept criticism and to learn from mistakes, striving to please, striving to do one's best, looking for creative ways to solve problems, being a pleasant and punctual worker, being a good team player and so on.

Parents make the mistake of thinking that this work ethic, and the self-discipline to work hard and study, is developed in the final years of school. Not so — the work ethic is established early in life, primarily by the example of parents and to a lesser extent by the example of teachers and the norms of their peer group — it is more caught than taught. Students who enter middle or high school with poor attitudes and application are unlikely to change in the final years.

Parents can do a great deal to help develop a positive work ethic in students from a young age. Work is a concept that children understand and parents can consciously develop in their kids. For example, a 2-year-old can learn that it makes parents happy to help them clean the house, a 3-year-old might learn how to help set the table, a 4-year-old to help feed the cat, a 5-year-old to help clear the table, etc.

Children from a young age should be encouraged to accept responsibility, not just to earn a hug, but to feel important because they have helped. If we can establish this attitude, that kids are to take responsibility, it would avoid lots of hassle about homework, it would encourage kids to plan their time better and to work hard to get what they want. If we can get students entering middle or high school with this positive attitude then lots of home–school problems disappear.

Parents can assist or inhibit the development of this positive attitude towards work in many ways:

DO

✓ **Do** give children responsibility and jobs at a very early age, as appropriate to their age and development.

✓ **Do** set realistic tasks and time-frames for children to complete these tasks.

✓ **Do** have positive expectations that your child will do a good job, whether it be housework or schoolwork or homework.

✓ **Do** have rewards for a job well done and consequences for a job poorly done or showing lack of application.

✓ **Do** help children plan their work schedule and take an interest in their homework.

✓ **Do** encourage punctuality, whether it be in going to bed, getting to school or getting a job done on time.

✓ **Do** give children friendly but realistic feedback about the quality of their work and effort.

DON'T

✗ **Don't** do everything for your child and continually clean up after them.

✗ **Don't** lose patience and do the work for them because you don't have time to wait/waste.

✗ **Don't** accept shoddy work where there has obviously been little application.

✗ **Don't** threaten sanctions or consequences that will never be carried out.

✗ **Don't** show little interest in their schoolwork or homework.

✗ **Don't** accept or allow them to submit work of poor quality.

✗ **Don't** allow lateness or disregard for routines and time-lines.

✗ **Don't** accept a poor effort without comment.

Study and exams

In today's world educational attainment is seen as the ticket to success in adult life. Retention rates in senior high school have jumped from about 1 in 4 teenagers to 2 out of 3! This is exerting pressure back down the line to get a 'head-start' on the academic ladder. However, our anxiety about their progress means that well-meaning parents often become pushy parents and turn the kids off learning.

Remember that our goal at this stage is to develop a good work ethic — kids who try hard, do their best, enjoy learning, become good time managers, are self-disciplined, set themselves some goals, can handle frustration, enjoy a challenge, can think imaginatively and creatively about a problem, enjoy learning cooperatively and not over-competitively, etc. Any child who can come through primary or middle school with these attitudes is going to be a success in higher levels of learning.

How to help develop good study technique
If the goal is to stimulate your children to work, then try these suggestions:

- For sanity's sake set aside no more than one quiet hour for reading, working and writing — preferably have a home rule about quiet work with no TV.
- Separate your ambitions from theirs.
- Ask for your kids' ideas on study style; that way you know and they know what has been agreed to, so it will be easy to say 'no' to pressure.
- If you are the family 'pusher' and your partner is the 'placator' or softie, swap roles and watch the change in your children's attitudes.
- Remember that anxiety is the second most contagious family disease. The most contagious is love of learning, so inspire rather than push.
- For detailed ideas on study tactics, essay writing and planning I still like Dr Fred Orr's revised edition of *How To Pass Exams* but my favourite, for lots of

reasons, including motivation, is Bernard and Hajzler's
You Can Do It.

Good study checklist

If you do want to help create a good environment for thinking and reflective learning, here are some guidelines:

- Is there good lighting, and adequate heating and ventilation?
- Is there good seating, and furniture to encourage good posture?
- Is there room for work to be left set up or half done?
- Can any homework and study problems be discussed with parents without fear of criticism?
- Is there too much pressure and emphasis put on exams?
- Is there a good balance between schoolwork and leisure and sport?
- Is there open support for what the student is trying to achieve?
- Does the family also have some quiet work time (for reading, doing bills, working with the computer, etc.)?

How to develop good exam technique
Second only to the mourning parents must do for teenagers over lost innocence comes the mourning and grieving over lost marks. If we're honest, few of us are happy with the kids' preparation or dedication as exam day draws near. Some of us react with a month's silence out of respect for falling grades but others of us are not prepared to let marks go without a fight. Both forms are camouflaged under the guise of helping but here are a few top test tips for better results. Write them out, then crumple them up or mark 'confidential', then leave them near the phone, in the fridge, on the floor, in their sister's bedroom or in the microwave so you know they'll be read.

TOP TEST TIPS

1. Get hold of old exam papers, swap questions with your mates — just reading your notes only proves you can read!

2. Get a study plan organised. Some start with their strongest subject to get revved up, others keep tight time blocks.

3. Tackle your weakest subject head on. No tears, no temper, but if it's no good, head for the teachers — that's what they're paid for!

4. Reduce brain weight — from book to cardboard summaries to pointer notes; a toilet door summary reduces the strain.

5. Work together — arguing a topic with a fellow sufferer or family member is one of the best ways to find out what you don't know before the examiner does.

6. Work to time pressure and write answers as if you were working against the exam clock.

7. On exam eve try not to cram — it just causes overcrowding — so just oil your summaries for efficient projection onto the page the next day.

8. Expect to feel twitchy on the day, that's the old brain hot to trot, just make sure it's well watered and exercised.

9. Outside the room ignore other kids' hype about no study, out last night ... that's called a 'loss-of-face' insurance policy.

10. Finally, when you're in the exam room, spend the preparation time working out what they're asking and how you can attack it. Examiners don't want your pat answers, they're boring. They want your brain sparking enough to keep them awake, so fire away. A good aggressive response will brighten up

> your answer and your mark and acts as the best camouflage for ignorance. Then start with the easy questions but keep your eye on the time; it will pass all too easily, but the point is — will you?

The best thing parents can do when it comes to exam time is to make home as low stress as personalities will allow. It's worth remembering that exams are the ultimate exposure, like intellectually streaking in public. I've known kids so scared that they couldn't control their bladder, their brain or their biro; my brother had trouble with all three. But there are a few simple ways to boost morale and performance:

- Their marks will jump by 5 per cent if the rest of the family is studying, reading or doing something quiet. Then at least they can concentrate without feeling deprived.
- Their marks will jump by 10 per cent if they're feeling fit. Keep only healthy snacks around if they like 'pigging out', and keep up their interest in sport or exercise of some type.
- Their marks will stay steady if their personal life is steady, so be careful about cutting out time with friends.
- They'll get a 30 per cent lift if they practise getting that information in, through and out — show a bit of interest in what they're studying; just explaining to dumb parents what they've been reading or summarising gets their thoughts in much better shape.
- If they insist on TV or CDs for company, then set up a deal that if marks go up, Mum shuts up, marks drop, TV gets the chop.

DO
✓ Do make sure exams are not over-emphasised; they are

178

merely another check-up kids have to have to see how they are progressing.

✓ **Do** make sure they do their homework. As for any test, the best preparation is just regular practice; if the kids have regularly done their homework they've done most of their study.

✓ **Do** give them ways to lessen their nerves. If your kids are nervous about exams then the nerves can be lessened by:
- taking a little good-luck charm or symbol of faith into the exam in their pocket
- talking to their mates about anything except exams
- imagining some super-cool, special scene that they really like; this will relax them and stop fast-minute concept crowding and confusion
- projecting forward in time and imagining what they will be doing after the exam
- imagining how a cool kid they admire would be handling pre-exam tension
- playing with their pet, as pets rarely suffer exam stress
- planning to get to the exam room early so time pressures don't add to the panic
- making sure that the home atmosphere is healthy and relaxed.

DON'T

✗ **Don't** place too much emphasis on winning or coming top, and don't offer bribes to come first.

✗ **Don't** give your children stress pills or medication that has not been prescribed.

✗ **Don't** allow last-minute cramming; a tired mind gives tired answers.

✗ **Don't** put your own expectations or needs for success on to the child.

CASE STUDY
Nicholas

Nicholas's mum first brought him to the clinic to test his IQ (intelligence quotient) because he was already outperforming the other kids at a prestigious private school kindergarten.

Right through infants and early primary school Nicholas continued to perform well, thanks to an encouraging home, books galore, daily reading and spelling with his mother, extra homework to speed him up at maths, educational computer games and basic skills drill. It was a full program but Nicholas appeared to be thriving.

The next time I saw the family, however, was late in sixth class, after his parents had had a dispute about why Nicholas's marks and class position had slipped. His mum was in tears and Nicholas was beginning to say that he was no good any more and he was refusing to do extra homework.

Once we got past the stage of blaming the teachers, his mother started to think about other possible causes and it wasn't long before we realised that Nicholas was educationally burnt-out. He had had so much competition and schoolwork jammed into his little life that he didn't have any friends and hadn't had the chance to enjoy life as a normal 11-year-old. What's more, despite his head start, the other kids had caught up and were overtaking him, and he felt he was failing the one race that mattered to his mother. So he wanted out. Mum's dreams had started to cloud his own.

Tips from teachers

- 'Don't force them to live with your own anxieties; practise good homework habits for the whole family.'
- 'Just remember that their worth is not determined by their grades.'
- 'Arrange a meeting with the year coordinator if things aren't working out, that way everyone knows where they stand.'

Drugs (including tobacco and alcohol)

Let's be quite clear on a few facts about drugs in the lives of young adolescents.

- Alcohol consumption and binge drinking are by far the biggest issues in adolescent drug taking.
- Young women constitute the biggest growing market for tobacco, while consumption is decreasing in all other sections of the community.
- Teenagers consume approximately $30 million in tobacco annually — but that's only 2 per cent (!) of what the whole community spends on tobacco.
- Very few children in the middle years are taking marijuana on a regular basis but many more are consuming alcohol on a regular basis.
- The marijuana being circulated and consumed in the community is many times stronger than was the case in the flower power days.
- The numbers of adolescents using heroin is very low (I'd like to be able to say the same for their parents!) compared to other drugs, although anecdotal evidence suggests it may be increasing. Still, in most areas it is not even an issue.
- In a recent survey of teenagers, 71 per cent admitted that alcohol is a major problem in the lives of teenagers — not in their own lives, of course.
- Very few adolescents will present themselves to a clinic for help with an alcohol problem, yet medical records of many alcoholic adults show a history of binge drinking as teenagers.

Alcohol problem indicators

These hardly need mentioning as most parents know the signs and symptoms first-hand. They include the following:

- smell of alcohol on the breath
- unexplained sudden onset of vomiting after being out with friends

- morning-after malaise
- unexplained loss of money from the house or complaints that they were ripped off
- overnight stays with new, dubious friends
- urgency of an extra glass of alcohol at meal times.

What to do
- Much and all as I don't like to confront parents on this issue, setting a good example in regard to alcohol is the best teacher — don't expect responsible behaviour from the kids if their role models aren't behaving responsibly.
- If you're concerned, confront them, tell them of your concerns and set up some contract on alcohol-related behaviour at that point.
- If they don't honour their own contract then you have a problem worth talking about to the drug and alcohol unit or to the adolescent unit at your local health services.
- If you're not sure what to do or say, there are a few

brochures around to help — for instance, 'A Merry-Go-Round Named Denial' and '10 Questions Parents Ask About Drug Use in Teenagers'.

- Research has also found that information on the effects of alcohol on the adolescent body is sometimes effective. Make sure that the school the adolescent attends has a solid core of information on tobacco, drug and alcohol issues in its Health or Personal Development courses.

Marijuana

Marijuana use is on the increase among the young. Despite the fact that alcohol does much more damage in the community, the rise in potency and availability of marijuana is of real concern to most parents. So here are some do's and don'ts for drug dilemmas:

DO

✓ Do lead by example — children have a remarkable habit of not listening to adults but are all too willing to copy our worst habits.

✓ Do encourage harm minimisation with regard to drug abuse; although many parents see this as a 'soft' option, by far the best, safest and cheapest form of harm minimisation is abstinence.

✓ Do base your relationship with your teenager on trust, for it is that quality alone which will arm them with sufficient self-respect to cope with the various trials and tribulations of teendom.

✓ Do have regular communication time for the family. The meal table is often a good place for random conversation about issues of the day. If teenagers have grown up being able to safely share their worries and experiences, then parents are more likely to hear what they're trying to say, or even what they're not saying.

183

✓ **Do** raise the issue at a parent–teacher night so every parent and the teachers benefit from collective wisdom and support.

✓ **Do** attend drug information evenings at your school.

✓ **Do** check the school's policies on drug taking and alcohol consumption — not just their penalties, but their programs to develop a drug-free philosophy in every child ... every school will have such a policy.

✓ **Do** be alert. If you have some concerns, there are several quite clear clues that illegal drugs are being used. These include:

- unusual smells and aromas, often covered by burning incense or perfume
- unusual paraphernalia in their room (e.g. alfoil, hose, plastic bottle with hole in the side, etc.)
- a locked cupboard or burnt matches in their room.

✓ **Do** check for any unusual changes in behaviour such as dramatic change of friends, drop-off in school attitude, uncharacteristic mood changes, money missing, etc.

✓ **Do** get advice from other parents who have experienced something similar if you're not making any headway, or seek the advice of the Drug and Alcohol counsellors.

✓ **Do** choose a time and place (e.g. in the car together) where you can get uninterrupted time and attention if you must front your teenager about your fears and worries. Then listen hard for a way forward that satisfies your worries and which has their commitment.

DON'T

✗ **Don't** overreact — many teenagers will have a go at a joint or bong just to say they've done it, just as our generation did with cigarettes.

✘ **Don't** try to go it alone — the reassurance and support of other parents is critical for your sanity and psychological survival.

✘ **Don't** believe all you hear — abuse of alcohol, prescription drugs and cigarettes remains a much bigger problem than cannabis.

✘ **Don't** base your management strategy on threats, grounding or other deprivations. While it's natural to sound off when you're hurt or upset, basing your whole management on negatives not only ruins the home tone, it destroys trust and communication — and doesn't work anyhow.

✘ **Don't** assume your child has a drug problem simply because they show symptoms which could just be normal for the teen transition to adulthood —preoccupation with privacy, secret phone calls, more interested in peers then parents, time spent in bathroom and bedroom, etc.

The Drug and Alcohol Unit at your local hospital has pamphlets setting out how families can help detect and manage a drug problem in their home. If you still feel there is a problem, let your teenagers know what you think and what you want to change, and if they can't or won't, go straight to the adolescent or drug unit for further advice. Meanwhile your job is to give them support and information and just maybe home bonds can replace the bongs.

Tips from teachers

✍ Teachers consistently suggested that if parents are concerned about some students doing drugs, being involved in alcohol, or any other drug-related issue, they should take the problem straight to the principal. The principal can advise what action would be in order after hearing and maybe checking out the facts.

Chapter 6

Home–school Issues

As we enter the new millennium, there can be no doubt that families are struggling. It is a fact that the rate of family breakdown is higher than at any time this century, with the figure approaching 1 in 2 marriages collapsing. The reasons are many and varied and open to debate — they include high expectations, attractive alternatives, 'me' rather than 'we' priority, more single-parent support, pace of life, separate careers, etc. One fact is clear; families have less time together now than at any other time this century — 62 per cent of mothers with school-aged children are in the workforce and the 1999 study funded by the government's Men's Role in Parenting Project found that dads work an average of 47 hours at work, that's the equivalent of a 6-day week.

While talking facts, it's also fair to say that schools are struggling too — not just from lack of funding but from lack of community support, from the diversity and divisiveness of demands placed upon them and from the lack of support from the families they service. Yet in every social forecast I have seen, schools loom as the key socially integrating service in the community; one recent huge housing estate development I saw had the school at its centre and homes looking into and hooking into this service, not only for education but for after-school care, computer networking, courses for parents and as a recreational centre.

School and home need each other like never before — if they can work together and support each other then we may well produce exciting and viable communities. If they pull apart then our kids and communities are doomed to self-destruct.

This chapter covers some of the difficulties teachers face and some of the difficulties parents face in dealing with teachers. In an age where communication is so important, it is vital that schools open their gates and make parents feel part of the school community, and that parents open their minds and get to know what the teachers are trying to do and how they can be of help. We start with a light look at the mistakes parents may be making regarding their kids' education, then look at what parents can do with some of the most common home–school problems such as disliked teachers, bad school reports, how to handle the parent–teacher interviews and what to do if your child is suspended or excluded from school. This review also looks at the issue of home schooling — how viable an option is it really.

Parental sins

What do you think are the 10 worst sins parents can commit in the schooling of their kids? That was a question I put to hundreds of teachers in my research for this new edition. I first asked a sample of teachers to list their concerns and then I randomised that list and fed it out to many schools (public and private) for the official survey. Here are the results, in ascending order of concern from the 10th most serious 'sin' to the 'top sin'.

10. POOR DIET — many teachers complained that kids come to school with no breakfast, chips for lunch, and then are edgy and irritable all day.

9. SIBLING COMPARISON — comparing siblings and how well their brother or sister works or went at school.

8. NOT ENFORCING SCHOOL ATTENDANCE — not only did that make it harder when they had to go but they lost contact with other kids and confidence in their work

7. FREQUENT CHANGE OF SCHOOL — this caused kids to lose confidence in school and also self-confidence, because they could never establish a secure friendship group and there is little continuity of learning.

6. NOT READING TO KIDS — this was regarded as vital, not only to give kids a love of learning and listening and stimulating their imagination but it also provided important cuddly time between parent and child.

5. PUTTING DOWN THE TEACHER OR SCHOOL — the effect of that was seen as much the same as parents putting each other down; the kids are caught with split loyalties.

4. LACK OF CONSISTENCY— kids will not become well disciplined if the rules are not consistent.

3. PARENTS EDUCATIONALLY UNCARING — parents who took no interest in school tended to breed kids with similar attitudes.

2. LACK OF DISCIPLINE — kids cannot feel confident and secure if the rules lack consistency, so they don't know what's okay and what's not.

1. PARENTS NOT CARING ABOUT THEIR KIDS — by far the biggest sin pinpointed by teachers was the devastating effect and the increasing frequency of parents just not caring about their kids.

I also surveyed large numbers of preschool teachers and day care staff using the same list. Interestingly enough, despite the age difference, it was surprising how consistent the two groups were, with the exceptions that poor diet was rated higher, and not enforcing school attendance was rated lower, than in the school survey.

I also gave both groups of teachers the opportunity to add extras, not included in my list, that were of concern to them.

Other preschool/day care concerns
- Sending children on to big school before they're ready
- Focusing on academic readiness and ignoring social

competence and emotional stability
- Putting children down
- Not listening to kids
- Not getting involved in the preschool
- Not providing sunhat
- Not encouraging self-help skills
- Not spending enough time with their kids
- Parents devaluing the role of play in children's development
- Insisting exhausted children not be allowed to have an afternoon nap so they'll go to bed earlier at night

Other school concerns
- Parents always believing the child's story without giving the school the benefit of the doubt, at least until the school side could be heard.
- Insufficient sleep — inconsistent bed routines and kids up late watching TV or on the Internet.
- Parents making inappropriate and excessive demands of their kids — not just in regard to school performance but pushing kids to excel out of school as well, merely to satisfy parental ego.
- Parents encouraging their kids to use physical aggression — despite the fact that their kids would break school rules in doing so.
- Parents who were too busy for their kids — there seems to be an increasing concern among teachers that more kids are not getting enough time to touch base and download their day.
- Parents continually challenging the school or teachers — teachers felt some parents didn't realise the damage this could do to their kids' motivation. When the child is forced to believe parent or school, either way someone is a loser, usually the child.

Ten Commandments to Parents for EDUCATIONAL SALVATION

(adapted from Rimm's Laws by Sylvia Rimm)

1. Parents shall honour each other (if more than one exists) and shall honour the school if they expect their children to honour them.

2. Parents shall model good behaviour if they expect good behaviour from kids — good behaviour by kids is more caught than taught.

3. Parents shall say good things to other adults about kids whilst in their hearing — what adults say to each other about kids has a profound affect on their behaviour (good and bad) and on their self-image.

4. Parents shall not overreact to children's successes or failures or the kids will come to fear the pressure to succeed and will despair in failure.

5. Parents shall remember that self-confidence in kids is developed not through indulgence but through struggle — so don't make the path too smooth or they'll slip.

6. Parents shalt remember that children must crawl before they walk — hand over the reins steadily and gradually over time so they develop confidence and self-control.

7. Remember that any family that is divided against itself or against the school will have children divided against authority.

8. Parents shall not invoke confrontations with children unless parents can control the outcomes.

9. Parents shall not protect their children from all forms of competition — competition is one important way children learn to achieve but over-competitiveness is one sure way for kids to forever feel inadequate.

10. Parents shall work hard to show how learning connects with living if they want their children to view learning as living.

Teacher phobia

Believe it or not, a number of parents verge on some form of teacher phobia — they won't go near their children's school, won't make eye contact with the teachers, assume that all teachers are out to get their kids and regard teachers as juvenile detention officers. For many, the phobia has been passed down through their own family, while others were given a terrifying time at school under the old concrete jungle regime, where only the fittest survived unscarred.

Education has changed; it's now a two-way process requiring parents and teachers to work together and support one another. Unfortunately, the attitudes of some parents (and some teachers) have not changed and the phobia remains.

How can you tell if you are suffering from 'teacher phobia'?

- Do you feel uneasy walking into the school?
- Do you make excuses not to meet the teacher?
- Does your child's classroom bring back feelings of panic or revulsion?
- Does even the mention of the word 'teacher' make you slightly shivery?
- Are you always ready to side with your child against the teacher?
- If you scored 'yes' to these questions, then you have disadvantaged kids who, research shows, will never reach their potential.

How to help yourself

- One of the cunning things that psychologists have discovered is that it's very hard to dislike someone who says nice things about you, so relay positive comments both to the teacher and about the teacher. For example, if your kids feel they're being picked on by the teacher, then explain it in a way that allows them to understand that the teacher may be under a lot of stress, and ask them what they could do to make the teacher happier (i.e. put some responsibility onto the child to do something about the difficult situation). If the kids do make an attempt, and things still don't improve, then let the teacher know what you have been trying to do and ask for their ideas and reactions.

- If you find it difficult to talk to people who seem more educated, important, assertive or self-confident than you, or who just have the ability to make you feel small, one way to deal with it is to do an assertiveness course or communications course through your local community education service. Teachers also suggest that if you feel you won't be able to handle a teacher interview the way you'd like, then bring along a support person to reduce the tension and help out if you get upset. They also suggest you might like to write out your concerns so issues important to you won't get overlooked at the interview. Teachers respect parents who've gone to the trouble of preparing for the interview.

- A short welcoming note to the teacher at the start of the school year, saying that you're looking forward to a good year together, gets things off to a good start that usually is maintained throughout the whole school year. This also helps the teacher, who may suffer some 'parent phobia' too.

- Become involved with the school in any way that suits your time and talents (canteen, volunteer reading aide, excursion taxi, etc.). This will help it to become your school, too, and will help you to get to know the teachers as real people.

- Never underestimate the parent–teacher meetings as a way of letting teachers know your kids are human (despite reputation). Before the next meeting work out what your children want aired, tell the teacher a bit about your child, and keep the conversation child-focused with the goal that by the end of the meeting you and the teacher have become partners rather than enemies fighting for control over education. If there's a major problem, make a special appointment to sort it out.

CASE STUDY
Albert

Albert was a farmer who was 'school-scarred' and hated teachers from way back. When he came to see me about his kids, he banged his huge fist down on my table and barked his disgust at the way these 'Godalmighty' teachers were now picking on his kids just because they had never done 'good' [sic] at school. No wonder they hate school, he informed the waiting room. I could see his point, of course — I had to! But the sad part was that any home–school antagonism can create confusion, enough to cause misery, divide loyalties and make grades fall.

In Albert's case we agreed that his experiences at school had been so bad that he was now reliving them through his sons — and that wasn't helping anyone. After a while Albert even agreed he had been badmouthing his children's teachers too much. As a new approach he decided to take my report on the kids straight to school and let it do the talking for him. He then stood up, shook my hand, grinned broadly and said, 'Good on ya, Doc, but I'm telling you now, if they don't take notice of your report, so help me, I'll job them!'

What to do if the kids don't like their teachers
- If your child really dislikes most adults, not just teachers, then they probably have a problem with adult authority and that problem requires immediate intervention with a professional psychologist or the school counsellor.
- If your child has a problem with most teachers then, if it's not an authority problem, it could well be a cover for the fact that they are not coping with the schoolwork, so spend your energies on dealing with

that problem, not on confronting the teacher.

- If it's a new problem, don't over-react; instead, ask your child about the good things that happened at school, how they tried to get on with the teacher, what worked, and what they'll try tomorrow to help improve things.

- Don't take sides with the child or the teacher — that just makes things worse. Give them time to adjust to each other.

- If you want to talk about a teacher with your partner, wait until the kids are safely asleep. There are two reasons for this. First, the children have to go on working with and relating to the 'ogre' you are unhappy with; second, kids have big ears — they love having news that will be attention-grabbing at school, so they will freely air your secrets as a means of boosting their egos.

- If a fortnight doesn't fix the problem, ask the teacher for ideas because, once their ideas have been aired, owned and implemented, there is professional pride at stake to make them work.

- Never call the problem a 'personality clash'. Teachers loathe the term because it often excuses the child from trying to improve or change.

- If there is still no change, the next step is to ask for a full assessment from the school counsellor and then to talk to the principal.

Tips from teachers

Dear Dr John,

✍ As a school principal, I can't count the number of times, when we've tried to find out why a student has a bad attitude to school, that we find that the parents have bad and bitter memories of their own school days. School let many of us down, sometimes it bullied kids, or it was cruel to them; education was based on fear, not love of learning, and sometimes parents carry those fears and feelings over and through their children. The school of today is much more approachable, it wants to work with families, it recognises that the family is the most important influence in the child's life. My door is not the 'office' of yesteryear. I'd like to think I'm available to parents at any time so that they can discuss issues before they become problems.

It is unlikely that the school your child attends resembles the school you attended. Rather than colour your child's experience with your own, go into your child's school, read newsletters from the school, ask questions and find out about your child's school as it is. In this way your children can enjoy the benefit of your experience of their school which hopefully can become your school as well.

Bryan

Difficult teachers

School is part of life, and kids have to learn to cope with the good, the bad and the ugly. Every one of us can look back and name at least one teacher who was bad news: those who stood kids in garbage bins at lunchtime, who were cruel, sarcastic, lazy or indifferent — among other things. But let me make it quite clear that we do not help our kids one bit by torpedoing their teachers. Especially as schools are very different places from those of yesteryear, as the 'teacher tips' principal pointed out above. Education is a joint effort; you can't sink one end of the boat and expect the other to keep afloat. Your child has to cope day in and day out with that imperfect teacher, and that teacher has to cope with your imperfect kid.

Remember, too, that the teacher's job is not getting any easier — we not only demand that our kids be highly competent in basic

195

skills, we want them to have good values, be well disciplined, courteous, safe, good communicators, fit, computer-literate, tolerant, motivated, and able to enjoy the performing and creative arts, among other things. All this, despite the fact that there is no more time in which to teach it all.

Does the teacher dislike my child?

Symptom	Possible reason
Homework not marked	Work hasn't been handed in; crisis in teacher's home. Teacher hates marking
Child kept in to finish	Your child needs extra time to work as he or she doesn't finish classwork or homework
Teacher always yelling	Teacher yells at everyone
Child comes home crying	Other kids are giving them a bad time; having problems with schoolwork; feels unwell
Child hates school	Child can't keep up but won't admit it; is being bullied but won't tell
School reports are bad	Child is falling behind so misbehaves
Child's work has deteriorated	Teacher is uninspiring; child is unwell
Child no longer tries	Child is being nagged; feels they are failing; family expectations out of educational reach
Child always in trouble for talking, distracting others or not concentrating	Social needs may outweigh educational needs; child has an attention deficit difficulty

Symptom	Possible reason
Did better in younger grades	Child is losing heart with harder work — a good home can give a head start, but that effect sometimes dissipates over time
Teacher is always cranky	Has teenagers? Is getting divorced? Has missed a promotion? Wants to leave teaching but there are no other jobs? Is renovating? Feels ostracised by the other staff? Can't manage discipline easily? Can't cope with noise? Is poorly organised? Is overstressed generally?
Child's grades have dropped	Different grading styles, e.g. this teacher may not give marks for decoration or good colouring-in

These are just examples. There could be many reasons for a teacher to give you or your child a bad impression which have nothing to do with disliking your child. Friendly communication is the best way to prevent little problems reaching paranoid proportions.

DON'T

✗ **Don't** assume that kids never distort the truth to save their own skins.

✗ **Don't** write to the Education Department before talking to the school executives.

✗ **Don't** change your child's school in a hurry because you may actually be transferring the problem, and the kids' self-confidence will suffer by losing contact with friends.

✗ **Don't** just assume that the problem will rectify itself. If your child is unhappy or is resisting school, then you can't afford to sit back and let it fester. Either ask the school principal or counsellor to sort the problem out, or

197

seek help from a private psychologist. Sometimes, of course, kids find their own answers, so talk about ways to solve the problem.

CASE STUDY
Ryan

Ryan had had two super teachers, but his teacher in third class just didn't rate in comparison. His parents noticed his enthusiasm for school was heading downhill fast and it came to a head when his dad went to pick Ryan up from school and heard the teacher bawling him out at the top of her voice.

Dad's first impulse was to go in and give the teacher a bit of the same medicine, but he knew that that would help no one. Instead, Ryan's parents asked for an interview and discovered that the teacher was well aware of the problem, but felt she just couldn't match her predecessors. This admission was all that was needed; after that Ryan agreed that the teacher needed help in getting to know him so one day he took in his car collection to show her and took in special drawings on another day.

In time Ryan and the teacher began to understand each other much better. Before long the teacher noticed a change that started to snowball. Ryan was up and running again, all because the teacher was honest and the parents were open enough to listen before they leapt.

Interviews with the teacher

Parents are often very nervous about seeing their children's teachers, whether at a normal parent–teacher night or at a specially arranged interview. It's almost as if they expect to hear the worst and become aggressively defensive. This shouldn't be so. We are all human and we all have a job to do — in this case parenting and teaching — which is one that we should do to the best of our abilities. So treat parent–teacher interviews as ways to learn more and share more about your children.

Even interviews about particular problems should be seen as a chance for parents and teachers to get to know each other better and to strike up a mutual, caring bond with regard to the child in question.

If there is a problem, either with the child or the teacher, here are some strategies to make the most of the opportunity:

Stage 1: Setting up the interview
- Find out when the teacher is available to see parents. Try to arrange a time when the teacher won't be distracted by other kids; for example, after school or during 'release' time. If you try a hurried chat over a running lunch then nothing will be accomplished because the teacher won't be able to give you the attention you want and deserve and won't have the data at their fingertips to assist the discussion.
- Try to write out (even in short note form) some idea of the problem so you can be prepared — and ask the child, too.
- If senior 'executive' staff are to be present, find out what their role is in the child's school life.

Stage 2: Clarifying the agenda
- Talk it over at home with your child and partner but, at this stage don't make any accusations, just gather facts.
- Write out your questions but gear them towards solving the problem (e.g. 'What would you suggest... ?'), rather than attacking the child or the teacher.

Stage 3: At the interview
- Remember that at the interview you are really an ambassador for your child and family, so dress with that in mind (decent casual gear is generally adequate and doesn't look out of place with the teacher's

working gear).

- Please try to have any younger kids looked after so you can give your full attention to the child's problem.
- Try to keep the focus on the child and the current problem. Raising an old problem from another year is usually counterproductive.
- If the discussion is too fast for you or for your note-taking then it's perfectly proper to ask the teacher to go over a point or two. As in every other occupation, teachers have their own in-house jargon (e.g. auditory memory, sight vocab, gross motor, thematic approach, integrated curriculum, outcomes, perceptual problem, contract learning, etc.). Don't hesitate to ask for an explanation in layman's language.
- Express your views confidently — let's face it, no one knows your child better than you, and the aim of most interviews is to help all the parties to get to know each other as real people, not just as student, teacher or parent.
- Try to direct the discussion towards steps that can be taken to improve the situation so that everyone will know what they are aiming for.
- Be clear about any strategies that involve you.
- Sum up and make another meeting time to review progress.

If a scheme like this could always be followed, there is no reason why everyone couldn't leave 'the interview' feeling a lot easier and more comfortable about the child, the teacher and the school. It's worth remembering that kids are the guaranteed losers in any conflict between the school and the home.

If the interview does not appear to be resolving anything
1. Don't be confrontational. Express your concern along the lines of 'I'm worried about ... and I'd like your help to sort it out'.
2. Find out exactly what the problem is, e.g. 'Could you

tell me exactly what's happening so we can find a few answers?' Be a good listener and ask clarifying questions.

3. Find out what the teacher expects and what they are not satisfied with — the greater the detail the easier it is to find remedies.

4. State what you want to happen by the end of the interview, e.g. 'Can we work out a way that could solve the problem for us both?'

5. Don't get drawn into an argument, no one wins and the problem doesn't get solved.

6. Get a firm fix on what is to be done by both sides and what consequences will follow, e.g. 'Okay, if Johnny does ... and I back up by checking his notebook each night, what will the school do to help it all work?'

7. Set up a follow-up appointment or phone call, e.g. 'How about I ring you at the same time next week to see how it is working?'

8. If things don't change make an appointment to see the principal or deputy principal.

If the interview becomes an argument
-   Say something honest but non-aggressive, e.g. 'I'm uncomfortable with the way this conversation is developing. All I'm after is your help in finding an answer.'
-   If the interview is turning into an anti-kid session, say something like, 'I understand he is playing up, so perhaps we can find some ways to help him improve his performance'.
-   If the interview is becoming an anti-home session, then say something along the lines of, 'Maybe we need a few home truths, but right now I'd really like to figure out how we can make things better for all of us at school'.

Complaints about teachers

At some time during your child's education you will be unhappy with something a particular teacher does or says or with their style of teaching. When we're hurting it's natural to want to take the issue up at the highest level, but research shows that 99.9 per cent of cases can be and are best resolved at the school level. If you have a complaint about the school then the school, not the Education Minister, has the responsibility to resolve that complaint. Usually this will involve the principal acting as the mediator but if agreement cannot be found then the principal may need to arbitrate. When making the complaint, first get to know the facts (not hearsay) and have some idea of the resolution you seek, for your child' sake as well as yours. Be careful not to get into a slanging match or blaming, as that just leads to counterpunching and a lot of hurt feelings, and nothing is resolved because emotions are too hot to handle. Teachers, like you and me, do make mistakes. If it is a serious one the consequences must be serious, if it is minor or a one-off then the matter is likely to be dealt with at the local level through counselling or a remedial program instigated by the principal.

If you need to lodge a complaint here are some guidelines:

DO

✓   Do know your facts.

✓   Do approach the school in a courteous manner — having a legitimate complaint doesn't give any of us the right to be rude.

✓   Do be clear about the nature of the complaint. Keep it focused and specific.

✓   Do think about what you want to say and how you want to say it.

✓   Do think about possible solutions to resolve the issue. Possible solutions should be reasonable, achievable and realistic.

✓ **Do** listen to the teacher's and/or principal's account and explanation. Never assume your child has all the facts and no other explanation is possible.

✓ **Do** try to reach agreement or resolution even if it is a compromise.

✓ **Do** put the issue behind you once resolved.

✓ **Do** deal with the local educational authorities if the complaint is substantially unresolved.

DON'T

✗ **Don't** listen to hearsay or rumour.

✗ **Don't** go to the local authorities or politicians as a first step. Try to resolve the issue with the teacher in the first instance.

✗ **Don't** threaten school staff, yell or abuse in any way. Remember access to the school grounds is a privilege, not a right. In public schools and most private and independent schools, principals can legally ban parents who are abusive or threatening.

✗ **Don't** generalise about the teacher or school in a negative manner — that will only make the school defensive and take the discussion off course.

✗ **Don't** rant and rave.

✗ **Don't** demand one solution (e.g. move my child to another class) as that may not be possible and then there's nothing left to negotiate.

✗ **Don't** assume your child's version of events is correct on every occasion.

Tips from teachers

✍ The general consensus was that a friendly 3-way discussion
with parent, child and teacher needed to take place to really
see where the problem was and to determine the best
solution.

✍ Some teachers felt that my approach above was a bit
negative, and assumed that there would be argument and
conflict—from their experience, good communication between
home and school always resulted in a positive outcome.

The bad school report

One aspect of education that hasn't changed is the 'school report'
issued after half-yearly and/or yearly exams. In many ways it is
still the time of reckoning, although the modern report is much
more 'receiver-friendly' and tries to be constructive. Now many
reports give teachers a choice of 'computer terms' to give hard
messages a soft sanitised landing. I would make the point that in
the modern attempt to play down competition and avoid
misinterpretation, many of the report forms have become so
vague that they are vacuous, and so complex that they are
confusing. However, regardless of format, parents who are in
touch with their children's schooling should get few surprises at
report time; if you are shocked or disappointed that is just as
much a measure of parental involvement as pupil performance.

School report management
- If you are going to be critical, be careful. One student
  approached his father with his report and another that
  was old and dusty. 'Here's my report, Dad,' he said, 'and
  here's an old one of yours I found in the attic … '
- The secret is to check the report for comments about
  the child's effort at school rather than their grades. If
  these remarks for effort are okay, then school is okay,
  and the child has done their best. The rest is really a

matter of fine-tuning and steering. Perhaps a tutor might help if grades are down a bit, or maybe the teacher should be called in to help if the grades are disastrous.

- If the child's efforts at school are not very good then it is essential to hunt for explanations. You can make children physically attend school but you can't force their minds to obey — you have to attract their attention.

- If the report is disappointing, sit down with the kids and ask them to identify the areas causing most difficulty and let them predict where they think they can improve. Together work out ways this improvement could be achieved and pencil it in on the report for reference at the next report time. You could formulate set times to work, change priorities or use a tutor— anything that will help the child taste success and applause (because these things are the big motivators), not punishment.

- But if the conversation becomes very tense then contact the school counsellor or the school learning support team as soon as possible for help.

How to handle the interview about a bad school report card
Before you interview the teacher:
- Read the report thoroughly and try to get a balanced view. Look for both good and weak points in the report. If you don't understand parts of the report get them explained before you go off half-cocked at the interview.
- Talk to your child and partner about the report.
- Make notes as you talk; under pressure during an interview it is possible to forget the things you wanted to say.
- Prepare any questions you want answered.
- Put your concerns in order of priority.
- Make your questions solutions-focused rather than conflict-focused.
- Try to ensure that both parents, even if separated, attend the interview if possible — two nights a year is a small commitment.
- Remember that teachers are human, too — sometimes they are more nervous than the parents.

At the interview:
- Take the report, and any old ones if you want to make a point about any changes.
- Find out how much time you have to talk.
- Let the teacher know that you appreciate the time they are spending with you — teachers have families, too.
- If your child likes the teacher, tell them that.
- If you have made a list of questions then don't be shy to use it. It shows interest.
- Be conversational — it helps to reinforce the fact that your child is a real person with a real family.
- If you have used outside tutoring then let the teacher know and reassure them that you would like the tutor to work in conjunction with school. This helps to stop the teacher feeling threatened.
- If there is a problem, ask the teacher what other

resources could be used to help.

- At the end of the interview be sure that everyone is clear about what the solution or next step in solving the problem will be.
- After the interview write out the answers to your questions immediately so that you won't forget when you are translating the discussion to your partner or child.

When you think about it, children will have good years, better years and not so good years — that's life. Even the not so good years academically can be real winners if the kids feel good about school, or if they do well in sport or music or in some other interest area. Kids' progress is never in a straight line, it is uneven; humans are uneven and it adds unnecessary anxiety to the family to over-react to every little trough in life. Just monitor their progress closely to make sure that the problems don't continue and, more importantly, that their love of learning is leaping along nicely.

Many schools now use the student-led conference in which the student, in front of parent and teacher, talks about the report and their progress and makes suggestions as to where and how they intend to improve. I like it, although it's more exhausting for everyone, because it puts responsibility where it belongs.

Tips from teachers

✍ 'No parent or child should receive a shock report — if parents consult teachers regularly, attend interviews and parent–teacher nights the report will be more of a summary than a judgment.'

✍ 'Before the report comes home, perhaps ask the students to write reports on themselves, which can be discussed against the teacher's version.'

Suspension, expulsion and other punishments

Virtually every school in Australia now has a behaviour code. It doesn't rely on the cane, it doesn't rely on hurting kids, it relies on teaching kids. It relies on consensus, consistency and firm consequences. Good schools have developed this code in conjunction with parents, teachers and pupils so that the whole school community has some ownership and allegiance to it — it's their code. Likewise every school system in Australia, to my knowledge, has developed well-documented and objective criteria and procedures for serious breaches of that behaviour code.

Parents who are in regular contact with the school through canteen work, uniform pool, parent groups, parent helper, working bees and so on will know early in the piece if problems are occurring and can prevent them ever escalating to the point of suspension or expulsion.

However, if you do get the dreaded phone call that tells you that your child's services are no longer required, you can generally assume that there has been a long track record of problems.

Occasionally, of course, suspension may occur immediately for a severe misdemeanour such as violence or drugs. In such cases the whole family should seek urgent help from a psychologist rather than fight with the school over its standards.

On the whole, it is probably unwise to try and handle it all on your own. If your child is heading for suspension then consult the school counsellor or guidance officer and seek outside professional help and advice. When you attend the school interview try to avoid any attribution of blame or confrontation; keep the focus on the problems and the plan of action suggested to solve them. If there has been some recent change in family health or circumstances, then make sure the school is made aware that this has occurred, because it might explain the child's behaviour and may convince the school to let them stay on until everything settles down. If the problem is a long-standing one, then get a full medical and psychological assessment. After suspension has been settled, work out what is expected and who will be checking that the strategies are working.

Every school system will have its own criteria but here are some general guidelines and procedures for suspension and expulsion.

Principles for suspension and expulsion

- All students have the right to be treated fairly and with dignity in an environment free from disruption, intimidation, harassment, and discrimination.
- There will be cases where a student's behaviour requires suspension or expulsion.
- Parents and the school community should be aware of these procedures.
- Suspension is most effective when it highlights the caregiver's role in collaborating with the school to change the student's behaviour so that they can rejoin the school community as quickly as possible.
- Suspension also allows the students time to reflect on their behaviour and to accept responsibility to change their behaviour to meet the school's expectations. It also allows time for school personnel to plan appropriate support to assist with successful re-entry.
- In implementing this policy no student should be discriminated against on the basis of race, sex, marital status, disability, sexual preference or age.
- School principals are expected to adhere to the principles of natural justice and proceedual fairness when dealing with discipline issues.

Suspension

- The principal may suspend immediately where the welfare of other students is at risk (e.g. violence, threats of violence, possessing weapons or illegal drugs).

- In other cases suspension would not be immediate but come only after all other disciplinary strategies have been exhausted, after discussion with a parent or caregiver about the specific problems and after a formal caution.
- Principals may also suspend on the grounds of persistent disobedience or engaging in criminal behaviour related to the school.
- Suspensions will usually be of short duration (up to 4 days) in the first instance but if such measures are unsuccessful the principal may impose suspensions of up to 20 days.
- If after long suspension the matters remain unresolved the principal may recommend placement in another school, or expulsion.
- The principal must ensure that all details of the suspension are recorded in a register with all relevant documentation.

Expulsion
In extreme cases a principal may expel a student or make recommendation to do so.

- The decision to expel may be made on the basis of either misbehaviour or unsatisfactory participation in learning by a student of post-compulsory age (i.e. generally over the age of 15).
- The principal must ensure that all appropriate welfare strategies and discipline options have been implemented and documented before expelling a student for misbehaviour.
- Parents and caregivers must be provided (as for suspensions) with all documentation and must be notified in writing giving the reasons why expulsion is being considered and where practicable giving 7 days for the family to respond.
- Where a decision to expel has been taken, the principal must arrange an alternative school placement or if such

is not available, other options must be considered in consultation with parents and other agencies.

Appeals
• Parents or caregivers can lodge an appeal against the decision where they feel that due process has not been followed or that an unfair decision has been made.

Please note that procedures will vary from State to State, system to system, time to time and from public schools to private schools.

CASE STUDY
'Mate'

'Mate' had been so nicknamed because he called everyone 'mate' and he was everybody's friend. Even though he had always been a bit of a handful, his parents never really believed he was particularly bad. They always claimed he was pretty well behaved at home and Mate was a good sportsman just like his dad so his parents didn't think his bad behaviour at school was a big issue.

When Mate was suspended his father hit the roof and, after threatening Mate, decided he'd go and sort the school out. When we became involved everything was at flashpoint and accusations were being fired in any and every direction. Mate had committed a few school crimes, the school had been a little lax about informing his parents, and Dad was really offside with the school.

A case conference was set up with the local guidance officer to work out some solutions. The school agreed to write in Mate's diary every week and he was given a behaviour card, which his father had to sign daily A few incentives for good behaviour were set up, while the consequences for unacceptable behaviour were clearly outlined. The sportsmaster took Mate under his wing, and he underwent some counselling. Help was also found for his reading problem.

Mate made the Australian Schoolboys football team, and went on to play State of Origin football and to win best and fairest player awards; he also gained his Higher School Certificate. Mate now has his football to believe in, and his dad can pick on the referees!

DO

✓ **Do** leap into action straightaway if the warning signs are becoming ominous. Set up a time to meet the principal and arrange regular meetings thereafter to review the child's progress.

✓ **Do** assume that your child has a problem. Parents who defend and excuse their kids for serious behaviour problems aren't doing them one bit of good; the kids never learn to take responsibility for their own actions — our prison inmates are living testimony to the consequences of that approach.

✓ **Do** look at yourself. Before you take on an angry outlook toward the suspension or exclusion, take a critical inlook to see whether the kids are copying aggressive or antisocial behaviour. They may not be bad kids, just good apprentices.

✓ **Do** let teacher/s and principal know if there have been any dramatic changes in family circumstances that might explain behaviour, particularly if it is out of character.

✓ **Do**, if your child is to be suspended, ask for the action to be confirmed in writing. Make sure that the reasons and length of suspension are indicated.

✓ **Do** find out first-hand what conditions must be met before the child can return to school. This should occur during an interview in which home and school hopefully can agree on what has to be done and who can help the family.

✓ **Do** seek an independent opinion (e.g. from a child psychologist) on the problem if the situation has reached flashpoint.

✓ **Do** ask about other resources such as special classes for behaviourally disordered children, for slow learners, or for whatever the problem is. There are also specialist teachers for children with behaviour problems in most education departments to help both the children with the problems and the teachers with their management.

DON'T

✗ **Don't** refuse to accept that your child has a problem.

✗ **Don't** set off for World War III — negotiation beats confrontation.

✗ **Don't** threaten to call the local TV current affairs team.

✗ **Don't** rush to the local Education Office or Member of Parliament. Use the big guns only if, in the end, you believe justice is not being exercised. Then you have every right to contact the Education Office as a last resort.

Detentions, lines and other sundries
Let me begin with a personal comment and share my loathing for 'line-writing' detentions. I can't see what it proves: the kids don't feel any remorse, all that happens is their hands get tired and they grow to hate writing.

But before we become too defensive, it is wise to recognise the limited powers that a school has, and remember that, where possible, it really is a good idea to support the school. Detentions can be handy for kids who roughhouse in the playground or need some cooling-off time.

If your child behaves well at home and only plays up at school, then it's a fair possibility that they are covering up either a school learning problem or a social rejection problem, and salvaging a badly bruised ego by clowning around. Check

213

with the teacher and try to work out a plan of action by which any improvements are praised and which uses different penalties that actually teach the child something to remediate the problem. This may mean having lunch at different times to the other kids, doing chores, checking in with the principal each lunchtime or, my favourite, practising good habits every lunch session until they're sure they've got the message. Some schools use detention to chat to the kids about different ways to deal with a situation.

Perhaps the most frequent misdemeanour resulting in some form of school punishment is talking in class. Some kids talk in class because they can't do the work; some talk because they are so insecure socially that they have to keep checking that the communication lines are open; others talk because they prefer the attention on them rather than the teacher or work, others talk because work just doesn't grab their attention; while still others talk because they have Attention Deficit Disorder (ADHD). This means they are inclined to act before they think, to be poor listeners, to fidget, and to shoot from the lip.

If this is why the kids are getting into trouble or being asked to write out lines, then talk to the teacher about other ways of beating the problem. It could be that they will have to sit away from other kids until they show that they can be moved closer, or perhaps they need a medical or psychological assessment, or there needs to be some work on self-esteem.

If they lack friends, perhaps the class would benefit from some exercises from books such as Helen McGrath's *Friendly Kids, Friendly Classrooms*, or they could deliver messages to the office (and choose a friend for company) if a whole lesson has passed without them disturbing others. Perhaps the whole class could be rewarded (e.g. a one-minute early mark or some extra art) if the teacher is pleased with their efforts. That way the whole class will assist rather than subvert the teacher's tactics.

DO

✓ Do expect to be notified about after-school detentions, if such apply at your school.

✓ Do return notes about detention and take action if they become regular.

✓ Do remember that your kid's version of circumstances may have selective omissions.

✓ Do talk to your child about their problems and help to find solutions.

DON'T

✗ Don't punish school behaviour at home; that is the school's role.

✗ Don't withdraw weekend sport for poor behaviour at school. Taking away the one good part of a child's life will only deepen resentment.

✗ Don't refuse to cooperate with school efforts.

✗ Don't criticise the school in front of your kids; that's a licence for mayhem.

Tips from teachers

✍ Most teachers expressed the view that there should be a 3-way discussion between home, school and pupil to sort out the problem and get some plan of action to rectify it.

✍ Some said that when children are suspended it's important that they don't see it as a day off — it's not a holiday; see if they can do some schoolwork while at home or at least some housework if schoolwork's not possible. Spend time talking through the problem and what parents and children can do so there won't be a problem when they return.

Home schooling

For some parents home schooling has become a real alternative to public or private school. There are many different reasons why parents choose to home school, including dissatisfaction with their children's progress, behaviour problems at school, religious convictions, concerns about bad behaviour or the influence of peers at school, some special educational vision for their children, concerns about the whole child, not just the pupil, etc.

Most home educators take the view that home is the most fundamental place of learning and parents can not only teach their children in the way they prefer but go on learning themselves as they prepare and teach material to their children. Some families home educate for weeks, some for months, some for years, some mix children's time at school with time in home education.

Some home educators follow a correspondence course, others work from textbooks, some follow State Education Department curricula and others passionately believe in 'natural' learning — with the education building upon the children's own interests.

There can be no doubt that this form of education is becoming more popular. Statistics I have been able to gather suggest that there has been a significant jump in home education over the past 10 years.

However, before disgruntled, disillusioned or disappointed parents head down that home road there are several key considerations. Home education:

- is not cheaper
- takes an enormous commitment from parents to sustain the effort over the long term
- does jeopardise children's social development and ability to get on with peers, unless home educators take steps to ensure that social opportunities are supplemented
- means that parents and children don't get much of a break

from each other — that may not be an issue in the short term but it can wear thin if parents find their kids stressful

- means that parents must keep pace with curriculum expectations if they don't want their child to be at a disadvantage if and when formal schooling is resumed
- carries the danger that 'education' can take over the whole house and whole family — sometimes children resent being permanent pupils.
- Unless the parent knows how to teach and manage behaviour easily and adequately, there will be problems in disciplining the kids.
- The daily commitment of time to the kids is a real consideration — not just to teach, but to do all the other child care duties and prepare material for the next sessions.
- Although not all home educators are registered (and I think there's a strong case why they should be), registered home educators will be inspected regularly by the education authority in their State — some parents may not welcome such intrusion.
- There is also need to find time to in-service and self-educate so that the children are not disadvantaged vis-a-vis their school mates.
- Some parents may grow to resent the lack of private space and time away from the children.

There are home-schooling support groups in most communities now and education authorities could inform parents of those contacts, as could the Internet. In this regard there are several useful web sites, locatable by searching 'homeschool'. One useful site is: **http://homeschool.3dproductions.com.au**.

Home schooling is a form of education that is not for the faint-hearted nor for those lacking real commitment to its principles. Parents contemplating such a move are strongly advised to discuss it at length within the family and with educators they respect, and to visit several other home educators to get the inside information.

CASE STUDY

Dear Dr John,

We are home educators and loving it. We didn't decide to go this way overnight and the arrangement is open-ended, so that if we or our son feel we need to go back to formal schooling we can.

Our reasons for home educating were partly religious, as we're Christian and were worried about some of the influences at school, but more importantly, we started to see our son falling behind and losing all his love of learning — he was a sad boy. The final crunch came when I went up to the school one day to take him to a dentist's appointment and there he was sitting outside the room because, the teacher said, he talked too much. He said he had been sent out every day for over 6 months.

Since we started home education we have seen big changes in him — he's much happier, his reading has picked up and we're much happier too. Although home education takes up lots of our day, we don't regret it one bit — it's just great to see his love of learning re-emerge. This week we've been doing volcanoes and so our reading, maths, art, research skills, computer time have all been around that theme.

We have no regrets at all and compensate for lack of time with school mates by getting Damien involved in the church Boys' Brigade and cricket. But my advice is to get in touch with other home educators first so you know what it's all about.

Judy and Rick

Latchkey kids

With more and more mothers going back into the workforce, more and more kids are going home to an empty house after school. In the 1980s they were called 'latchkey' children and the practice was considered 'ris-key'. The word for the 1990s was 'self-care', because research reviewed by the Institute of Family Studies in Victoria found that facts were more friendly than fears. Problems such as delinquency were found to be more attributable to chronic family friction than to growing up as a latchkey child. There is still no evidence that a well-planned return to work does any harm to kids over the age of 2, and there's plenty of evidence that it can be very healthy for Mum and the rest of the family. In the 21st century, with increasing global anxiety, parents will be even more sensitive to anything ris-key. They are already increasingly opting for work flexibility so one parent can be home when the kids come home, or for more home office type work for at least part of the week as technology increasingly permits (computers, mobile phone, networking), or to use at-school after-school care where they feel the kids are safe.

Nevertheless self-care after school (and even sometimes before school) is still a big issue for many households. It appears that how well the self-care system works depends on the type of child, their age, the strength and discipline of the family unit, the length of time children are left alone, their training in emergency procedures and self-care, and regular reviews of the arrangements. Every kid benefits from some time alone, some 'wind-down' time, but there are important considerations in making the decision about self-care.

Checklist for self-care

- Are the kids *physically* mature enough to look after themselves: can they change clothes, unlock doors, switch off alarms and cope with other such challenges?

- Are the kids *emotionally* mature enough to cope easily with being away from adults for the time required? Have they shown some ability to cope on their own or not to panic when you are a bit late to pick them up? Can they usually obey house rules (e.g. about the phone, fridge and friends)?

- Are the kids *intellectually* mature enough to read, understand, remember and carry out written instructions?

219

Can they solve problems sensibly? Are they able to take messages well?

- Are the kids *socially* mature and confident enough to get help when needed from neighbours or friends? Do they know who to turn to? Are they mature enough to call for help even when the problem is their fault? Do they get along well enough with any other kids in the house? In short, do they have enough common sense to trust them with self-care?

- Is the family mature and organised enough to know who does what in emergencies? To have talked about and set up emergency procedures? Will a parent be reasonably handy if required, and is there a work phone number available for regular or emergency contact?

What to do

Under the age of 10 kids should not have to be responsible for the house or themselves alone, other than in emergencies. But from 10 years on many kids prefer to look after themselves because it allows them to do their own thing in a nag-free environment. So here are some ideas to help them do just that:

- Train your child well about house rules, what to do if you are late, how to use a neighbour contact system, and what to do in emergencies. Some Red Cross branches have a local emergency number which can be stuck on the phone for kids to use when necessary, and Kids Helpline numbers should be copied from the phone book and displayed near the phone.

- Inform a neighbour or close friend who can keep an eye on things.

- This may be tough, but train the kids to read a bulletin board. On a fridge or whiteboard, write emergency numbers, routine reminders and any special messages such as 'Leave the cat alone'. But they'll never read it unless you add some good news — where you've hidden the biscuits for example.

- Make the place friendly with a welcome-home note put somewhere it will be easily found (such as in the refrigerator) and some company so they are not entirely alone. A pet of any sort that your circumstances allow is a possible substitute. Make sure you phone home at a set time if you can, but do allow some play time.

Many people, not just kids, hate coming home to an empty house, so give some thought to trying to arrange flexible work hours, arranging for your kids to do homework at a friend's place or at after-school care until you can pick them up, or organising some after-school activity or sport (but not every day) so that idle hands don't become a mischievous problem. It's a somewhat sad commentary on our times that so many calls to the Kids Help Line come from home-alone kids.

Kids' comments

✐ 'If your mum and dad have gone out, and you haven't known that they've gone out and they didn't tell you, you feel like that you are going to be on your own for the rest of your life.'
✐ 'If someone strange calls on you, you don't know what to do.'
✐ 'If I come home and the house is empty I just go over to my neighbour's until Mum and Dad get home.'
✐ 'If you are lonely you get your guinea pig and get up on the couch and watch TV with him.'
✐ 'If I'm in the house alone I just lock all the doors and windows.'
✐ 'If you are scared you go onto the verandah and shoot your cap gun.'

Homework

Isn't it strange? Two ordinary, positive Australian words, 'home' and 'work', take on a whole new negative transformation when combined in the word 'homework'! It's not just the kids who feel the pain, it's parents and teachers too. Yet in this age of information explosion, there's a real temptation to rely on homework more and more to help kids and teachers keep pace with progress. Yet at the same time parents and pupils are increasingly aware of how much there is to learn and experience outside the school curriculum.

All too often homework becomes a dread and a drudgery and a major source of family friction.

DO

✓ Do have a regular homework time.

✓ Do provide a set homework space, free of distractions.

✓ Do ensure homework is finished before any after-dinner play or television.

✓ Do try to get homework over early so it doesn't become an all-night battle.

✓ Do keep an eye on how long it takes:

- for infants' grades it should be fun and never take more than 30 minutes
- for primary grades it should not take more than one hour, preferably less.

✓ Do compare notes with other parents if homework seems to be taking an excessive amount of time.

✓ Do check with the teacher if your kid is having problems. Fights about homework every night must not be allowed to happen, because the long-term costs are too high.

✓ Do reward fast, efficient homework if your children are daydreamers.

✓ Do be near enough to help and provide guidance.

✓ Do check homework but concentrate on noticing good points. If there is an error, see if the child can find it first; if not, gently point out the error but avoid criticism.

✓ Do allow music, preferably quiet (e.g. guitar) or semi-classical, for concentration.

✓ Do make your kids feel important and grown up when they are working.

DON'T

✘   **Don't** do homework for them or it becomes a life-long sentence for you.

✘   **Don't** take responsibility for their homework.

✘   **Don't** use your help to give their marks and your ego a lift.

✘   **Don't** put pressure on them to get top marks all the time or they will hate the daily threat.

✘   **Don't** be conned by 'I'll do it soon'.

✘   **Don't** be conned by 'We didn't get any', if the teacher has said otherwise.

✘   **Don't** allow the television to be on during homework.

✘   **Don't** allow younger kids without homework to play nearby.

✘   **Don't** make homework time a family feud time — if homework methods are not working, talk to the teacher and/or ask your partner to help out. Your role is to be a parent, not a school teacher.

223

✗ **Don't** make them study if they receive no homework; if you want them to do extra work, talk to the teacher first for ideas and directions. Just reading to or with your children is a natural part of homework that can promote good vibes all around. For older kids, just reading for fun can be a fabulous way to build skills, imagination and love of learning.

✗ **Don't** focus on their failures — they've probably had a day of that already.

✗ **Don't** use the old 'in my day...' spiel — remember how much you hated hearing that as a kid.

Homework must not be allowed to spoil kids' natural love of learning. If it has become bad news at your place then call a halt to the present regime straight away — before you end up winning the battle but losing the war.

CASE STUDY
Matthew

Matt's mum had done well at school and, for her, getting good marks was really important. She had been planning to go on to university but an unplanned pregnancy had cut short the possibility of a promising career and housework offered her no stimulation (now there's a surprise). When Matt began school she took great delight in helping him learn. Matt's mother was thrilled with his achievements and merit certificates and started to push for more — to the point that Matt began to hate doing homework. Why? Because his mum was only happy if he did well, and ranted and raved if he didn't; the merit certificates were really more a mark of his mum's success than Matt's. I suppose the moral is if the coach does all the work, then the kid changes from player to pawn. It wasn't until we were able to separate Mum's ambitions from Matt's homework, and refocus her drive on self-fulfilment, that Matt was able to find his own levels and his own sense of achievement.

Projects and assignments

Projects and assignments are meant to give kids the chance to explore a topic in depth at their 'leisure'. Unfortunately, reality is generally a far cry from this ideal. Such assignments are a great idea if the project is well explained, if the material is readily available, if the kids are keen to do it, if there has been plenty of notice given, if the kids are well organised, and if there is some in-school progress review to keep the project on the boil. That's a lot of 'ifs'. In many cases none of this happens and the result can be catastrophic or comical, depending on how far you are from the next deadline!

DO

✓ Do work out a schedule with your kids to get the project or assignment done, perhaps on one of those whiteboard year planners so they can see the overview, as well as how the time-line fits in with all the outside school extras. For example:

- Step 1 Date to decide the topic
- Step 2 Date to work out where to get project material from
- Step 3 Date to collect material
- Step 4 Date to sort and select information
- Step 5 Date to write up work
- Step 6 Date by which they decorate the title page

✓ **Do** remember that disorganised kids need extra help with all the steps to complete a project.

✓ **Do**, if kids are reluctant starters, use the 'Grandma' principle; for example, 'Do half an hour of assignment and then you can have half an hour of TV'.

✓ **Do** find out exactly when the assignment is due and in what form; if the kids are unsure, then get them to ask the teacher for clarification or, if they're too shy to do that, let them help you draft a note to the teacher explaining what you need to know.

✓ **Do** help them to find material, but don't find it all for them.

✓ **Do** arrange for them, if needed, to visit the library or any necessary sources of material and information.

✓ **Do** take the line that the teacher just wants their best effort, not perfection, if they're all hot and bothered that it's not neat enough and they'll get into trouble. Often these kids will give away favourite possessions, CDs, time on computer, anything, to get the help from a bribing, conniving, smug big brother or sister. Modern computers have fabulous drawing, diagramming and often scanning facilities to help even the poorest 'pen-to-paperer'.

✓ **Do** check that there isn't some form of organisational learning problem that requires help. For instance, some children have a distinct neurological disability in organising their time and sequencing, or planning the phases of an activity.

✓ **Do** find other people who can help with information, such as Grandma or a family friend.

DON'T

✗ **Don't** do the assignment for them — the point of the exercise is for them to do the project.

✘ **Don't** do the writing or research for them. Perhaps you can help with the legwork.

✘ **Don't** let them leave it until the last night.

✘ **Don't** go over the top with expensive cardboard or fancy project books; an assignment is an exercise in discovery, not gift-wrapping!

CASE STUDY
Kristen

Kristen came home from school one day with the news that every parent dreads — 'the' project was due in that week.

Her mum cursed, while her older sister, sensing a chance to make money, raced in with her trading list: if it was on koalas Kristen could buy hers, ready to hand in, for $3, or rent it and copy it for half price. Grandma's life history, 'life cycle' she called it, was going for $4; Ancient Egypt at $7 and the early explorers for $10. (Apparently some communities have quite a blackmarket in preloved projects — minerals, gold, ancient Egypt, explorers, are regularly among the top traders.)

But Kristen's project was on the products of New Zealand and couldn't be traded. Her mother phoned another project-paranoid parent who hinted that there might be books in the town library. Down Mum raced in her lunchbreak the next day, but a quick check of the faces of all the other glum mums in the library told her that they were all too late. Fortunately a local travel agent helped out, so that night working on the project became a family affair. Big sister was the artist of the family so for $5 or an all-weekend wear of Kristen's Levi 501s she did the map and the title page; Mum prepared the notes and Kristen cut out the pictures.

Okay, Mum shouldn't have helped so much, but when all the other mothers are helping their kids, how can you disadvantage your own?

A week after the due date Kristen raced home with the good news that she got her best mark ever, 49 out of 50.

Her mum stopped dead, knowing full well what was in store for them all when the next assignment was due.

Kids' comments

(teachers and parents take note!)

🖉 'It seems as if teachers give projects just to keep us occupied; sometimes I put heaps into one and the teacher only writes "good work" or "could be neater" or something.'

🖉 'Sometimes I think that teachers think that you've got nothing else to do in your life except homework and projects. I don't mind a bit of homework but I also like the ballet and music that I do after school.'

🖉 'I don't think we should put names on projects because I reckon the teacher has favourites and they get better marks every time.'

🖉 'I hate it when you put a lot of effort into a project and you get it back and it says you didn't answer the question.'

🖉 'For most of my projects the comments on them have been all bad, never anything good.'

🖉 'I hate it when you have a teacher who you don't think likes you very much and you get a bad mark and they write things like "appalling" or "disgraceful" on it.'

🖉 'I'd done this project and I'd done about 8 hours' work and in the long run when I got all my marks back she said it wasn't even worth handing in and that really made me feel pretty bad.'

🖉 'It's not fair because Melissa's mum does all her work for her.'

Excursions and school camps

There are few encroachments on family sanity to match the school excursion: 'Where's the note, I can't go if I don't have the note!' 'Have you signed it yet, Mum?' 'How can I go wearing all this stupid stuff?' 'I won't need a jumper, none of the other kids are taking one!' 'Just drop me and go, don't wait around for the bus, it's so embarrassing when parents do that!'

Then, of course, the shy or sensitive or bedwetting kids have their own crises of confidence to beat. The reality is that excursions and camps do a lot to bond a group of kids together, to develop confidence, and give an insight into a different and, in a few important ways, a superior lifestyle to the normal rush and bustle of home life. And it's also a day or two away from the daily grind of school.

Most schools have fairly clear and strict rules about excursion behaviour and dress, so don't be conned about not having to wear a uniform or that no notification about the excursion was given; the notification has probably been securely 'stored' in the bottom of your child's schoolbag for weeks. If you are not sure about any aspect of the outing, phone the school and check. Many kids who have dressed to look 'cool' are left sadly at the school gate, waving after the departing bus. If there is a difficulty about the cost of the excursion, many schools have a special fund for needy families, available through the principal.

DO

✓ Do get a copy of the excursion note if your child has been forgetful; schools keep spare copies.

✓ Do put return notes and money in an envelope with the child's name, class and teacher and, if they are forgetful, put it in their lunchbox or pencil case. They're sure to look there sometime in the day.

✓ Do check the requirements for the excursion to get maximum benefit.

✓ Do, if it is an outdoor excursion, think about the need for sunblock and hats.

✓ Do reinforce the benefit of excursion education.

✓ Do ask the teacher to link your shy kid up with a buddy, so they will not be quite so scared of it all.

DON'T

✗ Don't rubbish excursions as a waste of time.

✗ Don't make your child do extra work to catch up.

✘   **Don't** be caught short about uniform requirements; being incorrectly dressed can be embarrassing.

School camps

School camps are a special breed of excursion and have the potential to be one of the most thrilling and the most satisfying experiences in a school kid's life. If parents and children are confident personalities, then camp is terrific; but if either the kids or their parents lack confidence, then school camps can become a frightening spectre because kids sense the anxiety and fear of separation, and feel very insecure about the unknown.

Before you become too frustrated or angry about your child's reluctance to go to camp, remember how many kids panicked about your own school camps, or how unsettled you felt. Remember, too, how many sad, departing faces came back as smiling, stronger faces. For many insecure kids school camp has been a real stepping stone to growing up. If your child is really petrified a few simple precautions will ease the pain.

How to help

* Make sure that your child has had some practice in sleeping away from home and, better still, sleeping out of doors — Brownies, Guides, Cubs and Scouts are probably unequalled for this type of experience. Even staying at Grandma's or at an aunt's without Mum is a good start. If your child happily sleeps over at a friend's house, your chances of them surviving a camp are good.
* See if the teacher has a bright brochure — a few real glossy pictures are better than imagined terrors.
* Try not to over-react either way if your kids say they don't want to go. They will feel different, isolated and inferior if everyone else is talking about the experience and they have been left out. Listen, share your similar childhood anxieties, and try to find out where the blocking is coming from.
  ▪ If it is from loneliness, then they must be 'buddied-up'

with a friend or two before the camp.

- If it's because they're bedwetters, have a chat with your doctor. Some doctors will prescribe the nasal spray Tofranil to beat wet beds but, strangely enough, just being away from home and sleeping in a different bed can often temporarily stop the problem, perhaps because the kids don't sleep quite as soundly.
- If it's just fear of the unknown, then invite other kids over who have already been on camp (preferably the same place), and really loved it.
- If it's because they'll miss Mum, then maybe let them take a little security keepsake, or write out what you will be doing while they're away, or get permission for a phone call if they want contact. You can even give them a map and draw a line from home — it never seems quite so far on paper, especially if it's a map of Australia or the whole world! But the best advice is to alert the camp leader about your kids' worries so that special duties or company can be found in a hurry if spirits start to sag. As a general rule, any camp up to 3 days in length rarely causes much homesickness — it seems to start cropping up on the third and fourth days.
- If they're scared of other adults looking after them then hopefully they will have had a meeting at school with those other adults before the camp. Parents are carefully chosen by camp leaders and many States now include a police check on adult volunteer supervisors (as well as camp staff, of course) as a precautionary measure and for further reassurance to families.
- If they're likely to baulk at going at the last minute, arrange for them to be picked up by a friend's family on the morning; that can prevent about 60 per cent of 'barrier refusals'. At the assembly point make sure they team up with friends: friends are the big fear-beaters.
- Be positive. It is more than likely that a much more positive kid will be returned to you.

CASE STUDY
Jane

Jane's class was going on an excursion to the snow — but the cost was $350. As it is for most of us, that cost was daunting for her parents in one lump sum. But the excursion was an opportunity for some real fun, friendship and 'fibre building', particularly as Jane had recently become a little withdrawn and manipulative. Her father set the ball rolling by suggesting, 'Let's make a deal'. He was willing to pay half if Jane raised the other half. Then they sat down to work out ways she could earn the money. They began with a weekly chore chart which could earn her $10 a week. They figured that this would raise half the necessary sum. As well, Jane and her friends set up a car wash to make a bit more. Their neighbour worked late, so Jane went next door any afternoon that the washing was hanging out and brought it in for another few dollars. A supervised garage sale of old toys and junk cleaned up a messy room and garage, and before long Jane not only had her money but a new ski jacket and a new brand of self-confidence.

Tips from teachers

✍ Some teachers felt that if parents knew the kids had a track record for baulking about excursions and camps, perhaps those parents could ask to be volunteers on the camp.

✍ Many teachers backed our suggestion for children to get opportunities to stay with friends or families as they mature, so the camp is not so threatening.

✍ Many teachers felt that ultimately it's not worth the fight if kids really don't want to go — discuss it with the teacher and let some school-based strategies operate, but don't force.

Computers

I do sometimes worry about kids in the computer age. I know that computers are the communication medium of the future; I know that kids enjoy computers; and I know that virtually every school has now invested so much in them that they have set up their own computer bank. But what about good old books? With pictures and print they can develop imagination, convey feelings, teach and communicate — but, when you think about it, so can computers. They can do all those things and play games, improve children's maths, spelling and reading skills, or assist with any school subject, for that matter.

I suppose I could worry that computer-addicted kids will become social hermits, but so can bookworms. No, to be quite frank, what worries me is not what is available for kids to use as much as who is available to use it with them. Computers are no substitute for parents and, just as with books for kids, much can be gained from them as a shared experience. You may have read the research that only 6 per cent of children's time on the computer/Internet is supervised.

Support computer use from a young age as you would any other learning tool, and be a guiding part of the whole experience. Use your parental intuition to make judgments about the appropriateness of software for your child. Monitor the computer just as you do the TV. Share in its use, strive for balance, and learn together. If you're unsure of 'safe sites' for kids use the kidz.net site referred to below.

Games or learning software

Playing in the sandpit could be seen as wasted activity time for children, but intuition and research tell us that this is a very valuable learning experience. Computer 'games' can be viewed in a similar way. What we may see as simple 'games' on the computer are more often than not teaching one thing or another — and I'm not talking about shoot-em-up style games here at all — so be patient, look hard, and try to see the hidden value in even the simplest games.

233

If you're on the Internet, take a look at 'The Children's Software Review', at **http://www2.childrenssoftware.com, childrenssoftware/** for valuable information on software suitable for all ages.

There is little doubt that the multimedia nature of the computer can make maths drill fun and encourage and promote all sorts of learning and thinking in our children. So use computers wisely to complement the learning activities that concerned parents have always pursued with their children, and don't forget to make time for that play in the sandpit.

The Internet
The Internet is like a bookstore with attitude, and CB radio without the static. There are all sorts of people and things in both places that you do and don't want to interact with. The trick is to learn how to use it effectively.

I'm not suggesting that you get your 3-year-old 'online' as soon as possible, but merely that you don't turn your back on this tool because 'it's too hard' or dangerous. The Internet is a fact of life, like TV and telephones, and children are as well-off learning about it at home with you as anywhere else. A new multi-dimensional, family-friendly, porno-proofed, safe site for kids is **www.kidz.net.au**. This index of thousands of sites gives children quick and easy access to just about any educational subject or interest.

Chat rooms
These can be great places for children (and adults) to interact with people from around the corner and around the world. Children and adults alike are drawn to communicating with each other. Parents sometimes have difficulty understanding the need to type information with a friend who could be telephoned, or with a friend the child has already telephoned to set up a time and place to meet in a specifically created chat room. Again, look at it as a learning experience; especially valuable when the children are bouncing ideas off 3 or 4 children from places around the world

at the same time; with benefits accruing to the child in reading, writing, thinking, and in sharing and respecting the opinions of others. But be careful. Real-time chat lines can become vehicles for sordid sport. Personally supervise or check that members have a security code.

Rules for kids' on-line safety
(adapted from the American code)

- Don't give your password to anyone, even your best friend.
- Never tell someone your home address, telephone number or school without asking a parent.
- If someone says something that makes you feel unsafe, leave the chat room or just sign off.
- Never say you'll meet someone in person without asking a parent.
- Always tell a parent about any threatening or bad language.
- Don't accept mail or files from strangers.

E-mail
As with chat rooms, e-mail can put the whole family in touch with some very interesting people, very cheaply. It can encourage writing and reading, just as we do with pen-pals. So again, use it to your advantage.

Homework
Yes, the Internet is a great place to do research and gather information. Children need to be aware of the difference between copying someone else's work and referencing or acknowledging sources of information. As parents and teachers we need to be careful that we set research tasks that require the gathering and synthesis of information and the application of original thought. It's one thing to be able to locate and copy 3 pages of information, but to be able to talk about it in relation to local examples, to apply the information to specific

problems or meaningful events, is another thing again.

Searching the net is an essential skill, and while Yahoo is the search engine we hear so much about, Google, at **http://www.google.com**, is probably easier to use. Again, help out and monitor.

A great place to start your interactive Internet experience is at 'The Global Schoolhouse', **http://www.globalschoolhouse. com.**

A quick look will give you something of an idea of the range of worthwhile online activities that your whole family could be a part of. Lastly, try 'Kids Connect' at: **http://www.ala.org/ ICONN /kidsconn.html.**

'Kids Connect' is a free question-answering, help and referral service to K–12 students.

Selecting a computer

If you are about to enter the market for your first computer for the kids, how do you know what to buy? Who do you ask? What do you look for? What do your children need? The best thing to do if you are really confused about the whole realm of computers is to save until you can afford to buy a real computer, not just a toy.

1.   Weigh up these points before you go and buy:
   - What platform (Mac or Windows) will my child be using at school?
   - Where/who is our main source of support for computers and what platform are they using?
   - Where will we be getting our software, and what platform might that be for?
   - Do we already have a computer in the house with a pile of software that we can continue to use?

2.   The answers to these questions will soon tell you what platform to purchase. Then go to a reputable dealer, and get the longest warranty available. Ask about after-sales service and set-up help.

3.   Buy a reasonable quality colour printer. Printers are

relatively inexpensive, printer cartridges are not.

4. Buy a modem for your connection to the Internet. You'll often get 100 or so free Internet hours as part of your purchase. Use that 100 hours and ask around about inexpensive and reliable Internet Service Providers (ISPs) while you do. Remember too that most modems will allow your computer to double as a fax machine and in some cases as an answering machine, so you may not need to buy a fax machine.

5. Negotiate hard for a range of prepackaged software that suits the needs of your family. You'll need a multimedia encyclopedia, or encyclopedia on line, as well as word processing software, at the very least.

6. Buy more RAM (Random Access Memory) if you can afford it, to help your computer run more efficiently.

7. Spend a few weeks looking in the computer section of the Saturday paper. Follow the advertisements from the main stores and you'll soon pick up on what the current base model computer is and what you should pay for it.

Software for preschool and 'big' school kids

There is an extensive range of software available. Concentrate on quality, not quantity. Be sure to have some multimedia encyclopedias, like those mentioned above, or almost anything in the Dorling Kindersley range. Check with your school computer coordinator and retail outlets for the best and latest. There are some wonderful packages available at low cost for children from age 2 (for example, 'Sammy's Science House') through to those aged 102 who are still young at heart.

CASE STUDY

Jason

Jason was regarded as a computer nerd, loved machines, just couldn't handle people; if any teacher had a go at him, he'd foul-mouth his way into one school suspension after another. We'd tried relaxation, we'd tried getting him to zip his mouth when he felt the heat rising but in the heat of the moment it failed him every time.

Then I realised we were asking a social misfit to be socially clever, so if computers were where his head was, that's where we had to be. Jason told me that if he wanted to shut down the action on his computer he would highlight the word 'Suspend', so I practised teasing him, getting him ruffled and then getting him to mentally press 'Suspend' and go blank to all the action until he felt back in balance. So far so good and reminds me that sometimes the best way to help kids is to use their strength rather than pick on their weakness. May not be a perfect solution but using 'Suspend' is one heck of a lot better than suspension.

Tips from teachers

✍ 'If children become obsessed by computer games, put a timer on and stick to it, any complaints and their computer time is lost. If arguments persist, switch it off and give them time to dry out, get out (doors) and help out!

Appendix 1

Recommended Immunisation Schedule

The following immunisation schedule is recommended for infants and children who are being immunised for the first time. This schedule shows all the immunisations that a child should receive, beginning at the age of 2 months. Parents should check with the family doctor for local details, schedules and expectations.

Starting age guide

2 months	1st injection of Triple Antigen (DTP) — a 3-in-1 vaccine for protection against diphtheria, tetanus and whooping cough. First dose of Sabin oral vaccine — this protects against poliomyelitis.
4 months	2nd injection of Triple Antigen. Second dose of Sabin oral vaccine.
6 months	3rd injection of Triple Antigen.
12 months	One injection of combined Measles-Mumps-Rubella vaccine.
18 months	Booster injection of Triple Antigen. Tetanus (DCT) caccine. Injection of combined Diphtheria and Tetanus (CDT) vaccine.

10–16 years (females only)	Booster injection of Rubella vaccine.
15 years or prior to leaving school	Booster injection of Adult Diphtheria and Tetanus (ADT) vaccine. Booster dose of Sabin oral vaccine.

Appendix 2

School Preparation Calendar

Term 1

January	• Preschool year begins.
February	• Casually talk to your child about school.
March	• Check Health Department Book on immunisations.
April	• Find child's birth certificate. You will probably need it for enrolment.

Term 2

May–June
- Make appointment with preschool to discuss child's development and readiness for school, especially if the child is young.
- If there are any difficulties, discuss any intervention strategies.
- If the preschool has any concerns about your child, it is to your child's benefit to consider the following options:
  - Make an appointment to see your local doctor.
  - Phone your local health service and discuss your child's problems, e.g. speech, hearing, psychological.
  - Make an appointment to attend the local health service.
- Tell the preschool if there are any diagnsoed problems and seek their help and opinions.

- Follow the program of activities the preschool advises to help your child.
- If you are advised that your child may need help through early intervention services, contact the Education Department's special education consultant, and keep on the case to make sure services are delivered.
- If your child does need early intervention help it is wise to advise the school that your child is having therapy.

Term 3

July
- Basic physical check-up by GP.
- Start thinking about 5-year-old immunisation.
- Find out about Kindergarten/Year 1 orientation program and enrol in it.

August
- Visit local school.
- Pick up enrolment form — have child's birth certificate with you.
- Tell school of any allergies or special needs.

September
- Make appointment with principal or the school's designated intake officer.

Term 4

October
- Begin orientation program.
- Pick up any information about school.
- Find out from preschool which children will be attending the same school as your child.
- Make yourself known to parents and staff through orientation program.
- Make sure school knows about your child's friends so that they could be placed in the same class.
- If the Kinder orientation program teacher is concerned about your child, follow up the suggestion by visiting your local child/health department.
- *Follow it through!*

- *Get your child immunised.*

November
- Go to orientation morning and find out all you can about the school administration, routine, teachers, school uniform and ways you can help in the school. This is a must!

December
- Go to any programs available to help parents find out about helping your child have a smooth transition to school.
- Read all of Chapters 1 and 2 of this book (or something similar).

January
- Practise routines of getting up and getting dressed, eating breakfast, brushing teeth, and walk to school if possible.
- Buy your child's lunch box, school bag, socks and shoes early — but before you buy check everything on the 'real' uniform (not just the school's wish list uniform), in case your child is going to look like the odd one out.
- Talk positively with your friends about the school and how you all expect to enjoy the new adventure.

Starting School
- Find out where your child's classroom is situated.
- Be available to drop off and pick up your child. Be on time. Meet the teacher.
- Give your child time to unwind after school.
- Encourage your child to talk about school, (e.g. who they played with, what story they had) but don't nag.
- Talk to other parents.

Guidelines for children with a diagnosed disability

If your child has a diagnosed disability (e.g. learning problem, ADHD, Down's syndrome, Obsessive Compulsive Disorder) check with your education department as to what needs to be done and when. In addition to those general guidelines outlined above, here is a guideline to help:

Jan–Mar	• Begin transition process as per your Department's guidelines.
	• With their guidance, the support team to help your child should be set up at this time.
	• Contact Special Education Consultant to provide range of school options and people to contact.
Mar–May	• Family talk with principal about child's needs.
	• Ask the Special Education Consultant if it is appropriate to visit schools if your child is going to be placed in a Special Education class/unit.
May–Dec	• Family to indicate school preference to Special Education Consultant.
	• Family applies for enrolment form for the school of their choice.
	• The school and family plan for the transition to school.
	• Child to attend Kindergarten/Year 1 orientation program.
	• Same guidelines as for other children for Term 4.

Tips from teachers

✍ 'I hope your book advises parents to follow up on concerns expressed by early childhood staff. Often we see this advice ignored but we, as teachers, have nothing to gain by informing parents of these concerns other than the child's welfare. Many of these concerns if addressed early can be remedied (e.g. by speech therapy, hearing tests, etc.) but they will become much bigger problems if ignored.'

Appendix 3

Placement Guide

Ages and Year levels

(based on minimum entry ages as at 1 January)

This chart shows the range of ages a child could be in any year level if they started school as early as possible and progressed at the normal rate.

Guide Only. Not to be used in isolation. Other factors must also be considered.

Age of child as 1 Jan	NT	VIC	NSW	ACT	TAS	SA	WA	QLD
18								
17				Year 12				
	Year 12	Year 12	Year 12		Year 12	Year 12		
16		Year 11	Year 11	Year 11	Year 11		Year 12	Year 12
	Year 11					Year 11		
15		Year 10	Year 10	Year 10	Year 10		Year 11	Year 11
	Year 10					Year 10		
14		Year 9	Year 9	Year 9	Year 9		Year 10	Year 10
	Year 9					Year 9		
13		Year 8	Year 8	Year 8	Year 8		Year 9	Year 9
	Year 8					Year 8		
12		Year 7	Year 7	Year 7	Year 7		Year 8	Year 8
	Year 7					Year 7		
11		Year 6	Year 6	Year 6	Year 6		Year 7	Year 7
	Year 6					Year 6		
10		Year 5	Year 5	Year 5	Year 5		Year 6	Year 6
	Year 5					Year 5		
9		Year 4	Year 4	Year 4	Year 4		Year 5	Year 5
	Year 4					Year 4		
8		Year 3	Year 3	Year 3	Year 3		Year 4	Year 4
	Year 3					Year 3		
7		Year 2	Year 2	Year 2	Year 2		Year 3	Year 3
	Year 2 6.4					Year 2 6.4	Year 2 6.0	Year 2 6.0
6	Year 1	Year 1	Year 1	Year 1	Year 1	Year 1		
	5.4 Transition intake Terms 1-3	5.6	5.5	5.8	5.6	5.4 Reception intake each term	Year 1	Year 1
5	5.0	Preparatory 4.6	Kindergarten 4.5	Kindergarten 4.8	Preparatory 5.0	5.0	5.0	5.0
	Preschool 4.0				Kindergarten 4.0	Kindergarten or child-parent groups 4.0	Preschool 4.0	Preschool 4.0
4		Preschool 3.6	Preschool 3.5	Preschool 3.8				
3								

How to use the chart

According to the age of the student (in years and months) as at 1 January of the current school year:

1. Select the right place on the Age of Child scale on the left, and
2. Trace across the chart to see the year level of the child's exact age peers in other parts of Australia.

Note: the age of the child is but one of many factors to be taken into consideration when deciding what year level is most appropriate for the child.

Bibliography

Adams C., Fay J., Loreen-Martin J., *No is Not Enough*, Collins, London, 1984

Appleby M. and King R., *Be a Friend for Life: Preventing Youth Suicide*, Rose Education Training and Consultancy, Narellan, 1992

Armstrong T., *The Myth of the A.D.D. Child*, Penguin, New York, 1995

Bernard M. and Hajzler D., *You Can Do It*, Collins Dove, Sydney, 1987

Biddulph S., *Raising Boys*, Finch Publishing, Sydney, 1997

Blankenhorn D., *Fatherless in America*, HarperCollins, New York, 1995

Covey S., *Seven Habits of Highly Effective Families*, Allen & Unwin, New York, 1997

Darvill W. and Powell K., *What Shall We Tell the Children?*, Hodder & Stoughton, Sydney, 1995

—, *The Puberty Book*, Hodder & Stoughton, Sydney, 1995

Dengate S., *Fed Up*, HarperCollins, Sydney, 1997

Donaghy B., *Leaving Early*, Harper Health, Sydney, 1997

—, *Unzipped*, HarperCollins, Sydney, 1997

Dwyer B., *Parents and Teachers as Partners*, PETA, Sydney, 1989

Hills A. and Stone P., *Good Food for Kids*, HarperCollins, Sydney, 1995

Irvine J.F., *Coping With School*, Simon & Schuster, Sydney, 1992

—, *Coping With the Family*, Pan Macmillan, Sydney, 1994

—, *Who'd Be a Parent? The Manual That Should Have Come With the Kids*, Pan Macmillan, Sydney, 1998

Kewley G., *Attention Deficit Hyperactivity Disorder*, LAC Publications, London, 1998

Lever R., *Guide to Child Care in Australia*, Penguin, Sydney, 1993

Lewis G., *Bringing Up Your Talented Child*, HarperCollins, Sydney, 1995

McGrath H., *Friendly Kids, Friendly Classrooms*, Longmans, Melbourne, 1991

—, *Dirty Tricks*, Longmans, Melbourne, 1999

Mullinar G., *Not Just Four Letter Words*, HarperCollins, Sydney, 1994

Sheridan S., *Tough Kids: Social Skills Program*, Sopris West, Silvereye Distribution, Newcastle, 1996

Van der Kley M., *Social Skills and Anger Management: a 10 session course for 7 to 12 year olds*, Silvereye Distribution, Newcastle, 1997

Wallace I., *You and Your A.D.D. Child*, HarperCollins, Sydney, 1996

Wilson C., Room 14, *Social Language Program*, Lingui Systems, Silvereye Distribution, Newcastle, 1993

York P., York D. and Wachtel T., *Tough Love*, Bantam, New York, 1982

Zimbardo P., *The Shy Child*, Doubleday, Dolphin, New York, 1981

Index

Other parenting and childcare titles available from Simon & Schuster